In Pursuit of His Glory

Maturing in the Image of Christ

In Pursuit of His Glory

Maturing in the Image of Christ

S. Bertram Robinson

An educational product of *His Vision Enterprises,* Pickerington, Ohio.

Illustrations by Creative Design Solutions, Columbus, Ohio.

Treasure House

An Imprint of
Destiny Image® Publishers, Inc.
P.O. Box 310
Shippensburg, PA 17257-0310

"For where your treasure is,
there will your heart be also." Matthew 6:21

ISBN 1-56043-289-6

For Worldwide Distribution
Printed in the U.S.A.

This book and all other Destiny Image, Revival Press,
and Treasure House books are available
at Christian bookstores and distributors worldwide.

For a U.S. bookstores nearest you, call **1-800-722-6774**.
For more information on foreign distributors, call **717-532-3040**.
Or reach us on the Internet: **http://www.reapernet.com**

Dedication

This book is dedicated to God
and to my parents,
Bishop Raymond L. Robinson (1912-1977)
and Ann V. Robinson (b. 1913).

Guiding Principle: *"The future will be great for the people of faith."*

Coleman Nathan Schiff, my "Rabbi" (1902-1995)

Contents

Acknowledgments

I wish to acknowledge a few people without whom this project could not have been completed. Most importantly, I thank God for giving me the desire, ability, and discipline to fulfill this assignment.

My deepest gratitude is expressed to my parents, Raymond L. and Ann V. Robinson, for enabling me to be on this earth. I thank my father for providing a foundation of love and strength. In addition to being my first teacher, he was, in every way, my hero. Although he died in 1977 of a heart attack, his spirit still challenges me every day to pursue excellence. My mother nurtured me and exemplified the woman of class. Throughout her life, including the present, Annie Lee, as we call her, has demonstrated that real love takes action on behalf of others, asking nothing in return. I am glad that she has lived to see this book become a reality.

I am grateful for the influence of Mr. Tom Evans, my college track coach and my second father. He accepted the challenge of taking an 18-year-old "wanna be" athlete and transforming him into a champion collegiate pole vaulter. He taught me that the real winners in life are those who set high standards for themselves and then endure the hard work required to achieve them. He passed away a few years ago.

I express appreciation to Robert L. Shook, my friend and mentor in the writing profession. Bob Shook has written over 40 books and is considered one of the leading business authors in this country. Although he is a busy professional, he has found the time to keep me focused on my mission.

I offer special thanks to Dr. Lonnell E. Johnson, Associate Professor of English at Otterbein College, whom God sent into my life at the perfect time. I shared the first draft of my manuscript with him, confident that I had produced an award-winning document. By the time he had completed his review, I realized that I had only taken the first step toward becoming a competent writer.

I appreciate the help of Jeff Garcia who assisted in the installation of my computer programs and to Michael Patton who tutored me for months in the use of my computer. Mike helped me to retain my sanity when, on one occasion, an electrical storm wiped out four weeks' worth of typing from the computer's memory.

I owe a debt of gratitude to Mr. Tom Bender, an instructor at World Harvest Bible College, who tempered the overexuberance of his students with the sound warning: "Don't go goofy." I am grateful for the friendship and counsel of Reverend Ernest L. Hardy. His courage and faith have inspired me to never give up! We will become more familiar with him later in this text. I have learned also from my friend, Ted Hill, how to look your greatest adversary in the eye, wish him well, and mean it. Special thanks to my "book title team" of Yvonne and Eddie Price, Ana and Mark Jackson, and Tami Robinson. I must express my sincere appreciation to the staff of Destiny Image Publishers. The professionalism and integrity of their effort have provided an additional blessing to this process.

Finally, I thank my wife, Dr. Deborah Wilburn Robinson, Assistant Professor of Education at the Ohio State University, who has served as chief editor for this book. Debbie has been both my biggest supporter and my toughest critic. She forced me to write in plain English, not allowing me to limit my communication to the language of the Christian culture. Moreover, she has encouraged me throughout and has sacrificed much of our quality time so that I could complete this project.

And now, a beginning prayer:

Father, thank You for the honor of my participation in Your divine plan. Be exalted in this, my labor. Bless those whom You have chosen to read this material. May they and I experience an expansion in the height, depth, and breadth of our vision concerning You. Energize us to faithfully pursue the purpose that You have established in us. And may Your will continue to become our will...in earth, as it is in Heaven. This I ask in the name and under the authority of Jesus, the living Christ. Amen.

Endorsements

The persons who have endorsed this text represent a wide range of religious, cultural, racial, and political backgrounds and persuasions. Their support is given, not as an unconditional sanction of my theological conclusions, but rather as an acknowledgment of the desire for excellence that has marked my labor.

"S. Bertram Robinson understands the inner battle one often struggles with in responding to God's call. For anyone interested in experiencing true shalom, *In Pursuit of His Glory* is a source of hope and a testament to faith."

J. Kenneth Blackwell,
Ohio Treasurer of State

"S. Bertram Robinson's book, *In Pursuit of His Glory*, should inspire every true Pentecostal who reads it. In addition to being inspired, it should move us all to pursue and secure those blessings that God has promised us."

Bishop Paul A. Bowers, presiding prelate
Pentecostal Assemblies of the World, Inc.

"S. Bertram Robinson is to be commended for submitting a scholarly and thoughtful presentation on an often neglected and overlooked part of American life."

Dr. Timothy J. Clarke, pastor
First Church of God, Columbus, Ohio

"This book is timely in its attempts to create unity in the broad, beautiful diversity we share as members of the one Body of Jesus Christ."

Harvey A. Hook, founder and chairman
Columbus, Ohio Chapter of the Gathering USA

"S. Bertram Robinson has written a powerful and challenging treatise for modern Pentecostals. He has provided not only insightful analysis and probing questions, but he has also put his finger on the pulse of the movement. His diagnosis should be taken seriously."

Dr. Cheryl Bridges Johns, Associate Professor
Church of God School of Theology
Cleveland, Tennessee

"Solid in its scholarship yet personalized with anecdotes and analogies...Highly recommended, not just for Pentecostals, but for all those interesed in advancing the Kingdom of God."

Dr. Lonnell E. Johson, Associate Professor
Otterbein College (Ohio)

"S. Bertram Robinson's unique method of linking the profound power of belief in God's Pentecostal message to the Kingdom of God, and the resulting comprehension of revelation knowledge that transforms the life of the believer, will be most edifying and rewarding to all who read this book."

Eugene Lundy, M.D., M.B.A., D.D., Th.D., pastor
Church of Christ of the Apostolic Faith, Columbus, Ohio

"It is a great pleasure to recognize the work of S. Bertram "Bert" Robinson...His sincerity and integrity has always showed in his work as well as his commitment to people and the causes in which he believes. I am sure those who will read and pursue the directions he provides in his new book will be rewarded with many useful insights and guidance for their lives."

John H. Ramey, Associate Professor emeritus
University of Akron (Ohio)

"I recommend this user-friendly book because it teaches Bible application in a simplistic way for an average Christian who must deal with the daily struggles for survival."

Reverend Stanley B. Robinson, pastor
Akron Apostolic Temple Family Praise, Worship,
Counselling, and Healing Center
Akron, Ohio

"Inspirational and informative. A winning combination...A great work for a first time author."

Robert L. Shook, author

"At last! A book that expresses what has always been in my heart. All ministers should read this book and allow the Holy Ghost to reveal that these principles need to become a way of life. Then God will be truly pleased and glorified. So, 'Let's Get It On,' as the last chapter says."

Reverend Hershel A. Strother
Maranatha Church, Carona, California

"I join S. Bertram Robinson in affirming that where we stand now, and how we urgently respond to God's call for knowing and experiencing Him individually, will have both immediate and eternal consequences for the vital contributions of the Pentecostal Movement."

Chip Weiant, Columbus-Metro chairman
Community of Business and Marketplace
Christians/USA Ministries

Preface

Since the inception of the Church, a level of tension has existed that has prevented us from realizing the full potential of our calling in God. Jesus said, "And from the days of John the Baptist until now the kingdom of heaven suffereth violence, and the violent take it by force" (Mt. 11:12).

As we approach the twenty-first century, The Pentecostal/ Charismatic Movement is now the fastest growing Christian belief system in the world, and it has the potential of being a tremendous force in worldwide evangelization. This book is designed to challenge Pentecostals and non-Pentecostals alike to fight vigorously against the cultural, social, political, and religious barriers that stifle the development of an inclusive Christian identity. In order to achieve this goal, we must convene the supreme court of our own minds and will, and issue a landmark ruling that in every aspect of our lives God will reign!

When I was a small boy, attending the Apostolic Pentecostal church where my dad was the pastor, I heard one of the "old saints" singing, "I Want to Live the Life I Sing About in My Song." Although I did not remember the lyrics, that title never left me. I grew up in the church world, living in the Pentecostal culture. And although I learned the language of that culture very well, my lifestyle did not match the rhetoric.

After years of muddling through on my part, God has caused that song to be resurrected in my life. Perhaps it was meant to be my song all along. It is my prayer that those who share in the reading of this text will be built up in their spirits and be encouraged to: "Run On and See What the End's Gonna Be."

Introduction

Incarnate. This is a familiar word for most Christians in that it is commonly used with reference to the manifestation of God, in the person of Jesus Christ. As the apostle Paul said, "For in him [Christ] dwelleth all the fulness of the Godhead bodily" (Col. 2:9). But what does the word *incarnate* really mean? And is its reference limited to Christ alone? *The Concise American Heritage Dictionary* (Revised Edition, 1987) defines the verb form of this word as follows: "...To give bodily form and nature to...to personify...to make flesh..."

Christ is the head of the Church, which is His Body. The Church is made up of persons who have been called and ordained to incarnate—personify, give bodily form to, and enflesh—the vision of God in Christ. Again, Paul helped me to grasp this mission when he used the phrase, "...Christ in you, the hope of glory" (Col. 1:27).

I believe that within the context of the total Christian ministry, God has designed a particular mandate for the Pentecostal/Charismatic Movement to fulfill. That threefold mandate is: (1) to recapture the spirit of God's redemptive vision as established under the Old Covenant and fulfilled in the New Covenant; (2) to restore to the Church the full complement of power, faith, and activity begun on the Day of Pentecost and continued throughout the first century; and (3) to help prepare the Church for the return of Christ.

Following is the major theme of this book: *We can bring Heaven's dreams to this earth, achieving the aspirations that God has for us, by partnering with Him in our everyday lives.* This is a book about life—the life of Christ revealed within us. To God be the glory!

The Problem Statement

God reveals Himself to us continuously in order that we might be able to live successfully in Him. He unfolds His glory in a progressive and loving manner so that we might partake of His fellowship and grow in His grace. I believe, however, that a large segment of the Pentecostal/Charismatic culture is not realizing this goal. Our theology is firmly established upon the Word of God. The outpouring of the Holy Spirit is upon and within us, and we are on the cutting edge of God's miracle-working power. But many are not realizing the dream of Christ's abundant life.

For example, a spiritual caste system has developed within the Pentecostal/Charismatic Movement. In some circles, it has become more important to gain an ecclesiastical title than to please God. Political abuses and hypocrisies still occur, and many leaders still struggle with sin. Family breakdown and mental and emotional stress are on the increase.

Moreover, the gulf of division within the Pentecostal family is getting wider. The need for the voice of a strong Church is greater today than at any previous time, yet public support for organized religion is diminishing. Although I do not know the reasons for this dilemma, neither do I share the cynics' view that the Bible-based lifestyle is an outdated concept; I offer no excuses for the condition of Pentecostalism today. Instead, I wish to issue a timely challenge to fellow Pentecostals and others who are currently trying to experience the reality of God's promises in their lives.

Where I Am Coming From

As a third-generation Pentecostal, I am a living example of the millions who have attempted to put into everyday practice the things that we have heard from the pulpit all our lives. Many have been successful in these efforts; others have not. Most have stayed with the ship, while some have jumped overboard, deciding, instead, to take their chances at swimming in the shark-infested waters of life alone. I do not speak from the perspective of one who has tried to live the "separated life" and failed. I am neither disgruntled nor unfulfilled by my Pentecostal experience. In fact, I am in some ways more Pentecostal in my thinking than I have ever been.

One of my objectives is to report on a sampling of God's continuing self-revelation during the present era. Some who read this statement may immediately think that they are being courted by another "Pentecostal prima donna," who claims to have just received the latest word from God. I most assuredly recognize that all such assertions are extra-biblical and, therefore, out of order. Moreover, I take seriously Paul's warning that, "...If any man preach any other gospel unto you than that ye have received, let him be accursed" (Gal. 1:9). All revelation that does not fit within the context of that which God has already revealed in Christ is fraudulent. It is clearly my desire in this text to, "...earnestly contend for the faith which was once delivered unto the saints" (Jude 1:3).

Furthermore, I make no claim that God is saying something now that He has never said before in principle, neither do I pretend to be the only one hearing from God. He speaks when and with whom He desires and no one has an exclusive line to Heaven. God's Word is one of confirmation and verification. What He is saying to the prophet, He is also saying to the preacher. I utilize this writing as a means to add my voice to the countless chorus of witnesses who testify to what God has been saying to every generation. In that regard, I have been given privileged exposure to an expanding volume of high-quality research among Pentecostal scholars. This experience has humbled me and has left me to believe that only the most arrogant and naive among us would claim to speak from a position of divine revelation alone.

My desire is not to preach but rather to assist in building up the Body of Christ. I trust that we will all be encouraged to pursue God's vision, knowing that He expects much from us.

Who Should Be Reading This Book?

I wish to speak in an informative manner to a lay audience of believers, particularly Pentecostals, who in their current struggles of life, might benefit from the witness of another "family member." In addition to my primary audience, I hope that this writing will prove to be a useful tool for pastors, lay ministers, educators, and others involved in ministry to the Body of Christ.

Although this is not the story of my life, the material presented largely reflects my own particular experience and scholarship. I have attempted to converge theoretical and practical elements into a sensible whole, and I invite each reader to examine, to critique, and to disagree. But please continue reading, for in the process, God will find a way to be glorified in us.

Textual Outline

The 12 chapters of this text are distributed among four major topical areas: Part 1 is entitled "Entering the World of a Pentecostal." In this section, the reader will pass through the doorway that leads into the Pentecostal arena. My observations and experiences are not necessarily those of a "typical Pentecostal," but they do offer one person's "Pentecostal-based" view of the world.

Chapter 1, "It's All About Time," summarizes the dynamic challenge to the Church in pushing forward the Kingdom of God. In addressing the current state of Christianity and the Pentecostal/Charismatic Movement, this chapter challenges Pentecostals, in particular, to take steps that will help unify the Church. Chapter 2 is entitled "Learning to Walk My Talk." It presents a synoptic look at some of the realistic and often inconsistent steps that I have taken in my experience both as a man and as a Pentecostal. This chapter emphasizes some of the naturalistic aspects to spiritual living or, to state it bluntly, even though we may speak with tongues of heavenly fire, we will still walk with feet of clay. The third chapter, "An Assignment From the Father," offers a straightforward description of the self-discipline and hard work that were involved in completing this text. This experience has caused me to echo the sentiments of the apostle James: "For as the body without the spirit is dead, so faith without works is dead also" (Jas. 2:26).

Part 2 of the text is entitled "Understanding the Pentecostal Perspective." This section is designed to develop a clear overview of the Pentecostal paradigm. Chapter 4, "What Meaneth This?" provides a descriptive summary of the twentieth-century Pentecostal/Charismatic Movement, detailing the primary world view, major tenets, and lifestyle of those within this particular religious culture. In Chapter 5, "Going Back to the Old Landmark," we shall trace modern Pentecostalism's historical roots back to the birth of Judaism in the Old Testament and to the birth of the Church in the Book of Acts. As we shall see, The Pentecostal/Charismatic Movement has evolved naturally from a rich biblical heritage.

The purpose of Part 3, "Rebuilding the Broken Walls of Pentecostalism," is to build a better understanding of the practical obstacles that must be overcome if the Pentecostal/Charismatic Movement is to reach its full potential. Beginning with Chapter 6, "So What Happens After We Speak in Tongues?" we shall examine what appears to be a clear mandate from God that, after we experience the baptism in the Holy Spirit, we must demonstrate the life-changing effects of this event in our daily lives. Holy Spirit baptism is designed not to give us a temporary "spiritual high," but rather to place us into the very heart of Christ and empower us to be like Him. Chapter 7, "Pentecostalism: A House Divided," exposes the separatist spirit that divides the Pentecostal/Charismatic Movement into distinctive cultural, racial, and ethnic groupings. The result has been the development of various unique interpretations of what it means to be saved and spirit-filled. The human tendency to take God's free gifts and entangle them in social and political bonds is clearly outlined.

The final section of the text, Part 4, is entitled, "Advancing the Kingdom of God." It is at this point that we shall move beyond the problem-identification phase and into the process of building solutions. In Chapter 8, "The Glory of the Latter House," we shall identify the characteristics of "God's Overcomers," those who have received Holy Spirit baptism as an infusion of God's life-changing, world-witnessing, and satan-defeating power, and who are putting it into daily practice.

Chapter 9 entitled "Know God" presents the first of four prerequisite strategies for waging successful spiritual warfare. In the exemplary lives of two figures—one historical and the other contemporary, we shall examine the distinction between knowing about God and developing intimate fellowship with Him. In Chapter 10, "Live in the Will of God," we shall review the basic biblical provisions of God's "Last Will and Testament," noting that, within the Old and New Covenants, He has revealed the eternal inheritance promised to those who are in fellowship with Him. Chapter 11 is entitled "Seek First the Kingdom Of God." Although the term, *Kingdom of God*, is mentioned only in the New Testament, it finds its origin within the Old Testament canon. And though the Kingdom of God is never specifically defined in Scripture, it is demonstrated fully in the life, ministry, and obedience of Jesus Christ.

The final chapter of the text, "Let's Get It On!" examines the ongoing spiritual struggle between the Church and the kingdoms of darkness. We are challenged to actively engage in warlike pursuit of God's will in our lives. Throughout the earth today, the Kingdom of God is a partial reality, both within the Church and in the lives of believers. But in the ages to come, we, too, shall see the fufillment of the revelation that John saw: "…The kingdoms of this world are become the kingdoms of our Lord, and of His Christ; and He shall reign for ever and ever" (Rev. 11:15).

Two study aides are provided that will enhance and facilitate the use of this text. First, a list of challenge questions appears at the end of each chapter in order to stimulate further examination and study. Second, a glossary is provided as an aid for navigating the waters of the Pentecostal/Charismatic language and culture.

Theological Foundation

This text fits into the related fields of Systematic and Practical Theology. "Theology, simply defined, is a study of God and His relationship to all that He has created" (Horton 1973, 46). It may also refer to the study of biblical teachings in general.

Systematic Theology, a specific discipline within the larger theological arena, is the process by which official statements of belief regarding Scripture (*hermeneutics*) are developed for use in guiding the practice of a particular faith. Dr. Stanley Horton defines hermeneutics as "the theory of the meaning of a [scriptural] passage, including analysis of the text, its intentionality, its context, its content, and the customs and culture of the human author" (Burgess, McGee, and Alexander 1988, 646-647). Obviously, official statements produced from a given scriptural analysis are based upon the world view of those studying the data.

Practical Theology depends on Systematic Theology for its baseline information, allowing the data in a stated belief system to be translated into a framework for everyday living. Practical Theology may simply be called "methods for practicing one's faith." It is at this level that we begin to see theology at work. When sacred beliefs become written down as doctrines, and those doctrines become stated as rules of practice (praxis), an institutionalized religious movement evolves.

Typically, organizational leaders in most denominations develop guidelines that are designed to regulate the behavior of their constituencies. But many of the faithful, regardless of denomination, still ask, "How do I make my theology work?" This text addresses in part that question.

The Bible-Based World View

Through a disciplined examination of God's Word, we can better understand His character and purpose. For example, in the Judeo-Christian culture, the Bible is considered the *written Word of God*. As such, it is the standard for all faith. Most Bible-based theology proclaims that God exists, self-contained and independent. The belief is also held that He loves mankind unconditionally and that He has executed a plan whereby all who desire may have intimate fellowship with Him.

But it is not enough that we claim to be "Bible read, and Bible bred, and when we die, we'll be Bible dead." In using God's Word as our factual reference, our spiritual world view (the reality that we construct concerning God) must conform to and be confirmed by the Holy Scriptures. We are responsible for bringing each claim that we make about God into alignment with what the Bible says. An erroneous doctrine can kill our faith and alienate us from God.

Therefore, what we do with the Bible strongly affects what it will do in us.

It is my belief that much of what we call "theology" today is nothing more than man-made philosophy, wearing a sacred mask and posing as religious thought. As such, it has no relevance to God. Too frequently, in testing some hypothesis we have about God, we go to the Bible or to some other sacred document, searching out those statements that seem to confirm our ideas. In doing so, we are requiring that the Scriptures prove us right, instead of allowing them to change us and make us right.

This type of examination yields a *particularistic* interpretation of God's Word and holds hostage the Holy Spirit, who is responsible for revealing God's character to us. God's glory and majesty will be manifested in us to the extent that His vision and His confession become ours. Individually, our commitment must be this: "God, I desire your will to be performed in my life, as it is now being performed without obstruction in Heaven."

References:

Burgess, Stanley M., Gary B. Mcgee, and Patrick H. Alexander, eds. *Dictionary of Pentecostal and Charismatic Movements*. Grand Rapids, MI: Zondervan Publishing House, 1988.

The Concise American Heritage Dictionary, Rev. ed. Boston, MA: Houghton Mifflin Company, 1987. S.V. "incarnate."

Horton, Stanley M., ed., *Systematic Theology: A Pentecostal Perspective*. Springfield, MO: Logion Press, 1994.

Part 1

Entering the World of a Pentecostal

The Spirit itself beareth witness with our spirit, that we are the children of God (Romans 8:16).

Chapter 1

It's All About Time

Woe to the inhabitants of the earth and of the sea! for the devil is come down unto you, having great wrath, because he knoweth that he hath but a short time (Revelation 12:12b).

A New Year Begins

As I watched the televised celebration in New York's Times Square that ushered in 1996, I was struck by my own realization that the world is literally racing into the twenty-first century. Most of the five billion people on this planet are probably hoping that the year 2,000 will turn the page toward an era of greater peace and good will.

Many Christians, particularly Pentecostals, feel strongly that we are in the preparatory stages of God's final work among humankind. A basic Pentecostal argument is that Heaven's eternal time clock is ticking toward the greatest event in history...the return of Jesus Christ, God's Messiah. From this perspective, we tend to interpret today's conditions as a signal that our present age is drawing to a close.

The Signs of the Times

For many, the signs appear to be clear: Crime is rampant in every major city in the world. Drug and substance abuse is increasing. The same is true of the AIDS epidemic and Third World hunger and disease. Acid rain and natural disasters, such as earthquakes, floods, and forest fires abound. There are wars and rumors of wars, with daily reports of growing political, ethnic, and racial conflicts.

In addition, a continuing wave of fanatical behavior is sweeping through the so-called *civilized* world. Much of this activity is generated by people claiming to be driven by some divine call to purify their racial or ethnic group. We, in the Western world, have seen daily televised accounts of the internal cleansings and barbarism in Iraq, Mogadishu, Bosnia-Herzegovina, Rwanda, Haiti, Somalia, and in the former Soviet Union; and using our own rationalistic thinking, we have concluded that these events are a reflection of life within less humanized environments.

This explanation was shown to be quite inadequate when, on November 3, 1995, the world community was brought to its knees by the assassination of Yitzhak Rabin, the Israeli Prime Minister. His killer, a 25-year-old Jewish law student, claimed to be acting in direct accordance with the will of God. This and the other situations mentioned above give testimony to the fact that, at least for the present, satan is alive and well and that the forces of hell are still hard at work. Unless humankind is willing to seek God's face and to come under His rule and governance, we remain vulnerable to an otherwise chaotic existence.

The situation in our own country is not so good either. In America over the last three decades, we have witnessed the assassination of one President and the forced resignation of another. Public confidence in government officials is at an all-time low. The Oklahoma City bombings, Susan Smith's murder of her two children, and the O.J. Simpson trial have stretched our sensitivities to the limit, causing us to develop a sense of lingering distrust.

The above list could be expanded such that it could be said, "We are living in the last of the last days." The apostle Paul, perhaps envisioning the days in which we are now living, warned that we should "...walk circumspectly, not as fools, but as wise, redeeming the time, because the days are evil" (Eph. 5:15-16). This, too, could be interpreted as a warning that it is about time for us to meet the Lord.

Most Christians would probably say, "That's just the way it is in the world of unbelievers." And as we read the "signs of the times," our prepackaged explanation of the future goes something like this: "We are now perhaps a heartbeat away from the moment when Jesus leaves His position at the right hand of the Father, steps onto the clouds, and makes His intrusive entry into the earth's atmosphere."

After a brief pause and a quick gulp for air, our sermon would continue: "Jesus could be rising at this moment from His seat of authority, putting on His earthly attire, and shuffling anxiously about the throne room of Heaven. He could be assembling the trumpet player and the angelic host to announce His climactic appearance on this planet." And then, in typical evangelistic fashion, we would end our sermon with the assurance to all believers that Christ's return will, of course, begin a series of cataclysmic events, including the Rapture ("catching away") of the Church (see Rom. 8:23; 1 Cor. 15:51-52; 1 Thess. 4:16-18; Titus 2:13), the Great Tribulation (see Dan. 12:1; Mt. 24:21-30; Rev. 3:10), and the Millennial Reign of Christ (see Zech. 14:5; Mt. 19:28; Rev. 19:11-14; 20:1-6). "Amen." And again, all the people said, "Amen."

But wait. Let's not pass out the offering plates just yet. Let's not start the victory dance right now. For, before we get too excited or depressed—whichever we choose—we might want to take another look. First of all, if this is truly the last phase of the "Age of Grace," then the Church cannot afford to sit down and smugly think that, as long as we are saved, that is all that really matters. Second, if conditions really are as bad as they seem, then instead of us crawling into some ecclesiastical bomb shelter, we need to get ready for a different kind of warfare.

As things continue to heat up, and they will, and as we get closer to the day of Christ's return, the Kingdom of God will wage a forceful assault against the kingdoms of darkness like none before it. Obviously, some will be better prepared for this encounter than others. With this in mind, it would be wise for us as Christians to take a look in the mirror and see what type of spiritual condition we are in.

Are we a lean, mean, fighting machine, ready to trample underfoot the total forces of darkness? Or have we developed a spiritual midriff bulge, the result of becoming a little too comfortable with the world the way it is? Is our countenance one of sincere dedication to the things of God, or do we have a few wrinkles on our evangelical happy faces because we care too much about keeping up with the Joneses? Let us take a quick peek in the mirror. A longer gaze might make us sad.

The Church "Sort Of" Triumphant

Many would proudly state that the Church, the so-called "Bride of Christ," is healthier than she has ever been. For instance, almost half of all Americans are attending church services and church membership is growing. What's more, worldwide satellite hookups are now allowing televangelists to drop spiritual A-bombs on every corner of the earth. So we should probably be pretty proud of ourselves, right? Let us look a little closer.

Charles Colson, in his book, *The Body: Being Light in Darkness*, has analyzed the current trends in American Christianity, and some of his findings are sobering. For example, he reports on a Gallup survey that compared the behavior of the churched and the unchurched in the following categories: people who called in sick when they weren't, who puffed up their resumés, who cheated on tax deductions. The results of this survey showed that there appears to be, "...little difference in the ethical views and behavior of the churched and unchurched" (Colson 1992, 31).

Second, Dr. Colson describes the modern church as an institution that operates on every level as a corporate enterprise, rather than as a dynamic body of believers who are committed to share the burden of Christ for a lost world. He states:

> "For most of us the church is the building where we assemble to worship; its ministries are the programs that we get involved in; its mission is to meet the needs of its parishioners; and its servants are the professional clergy we hire to shepherd us" (Colson 1992, 31).

Even more startling is the prevailing attitude among the clergy regarding this state of affairs. Colson reports on a recent survey that was conducted among Evangelical pastors:

"When asked how Christ would rate their church if He were to return today, less than 1 percent queried said that He would rate them as highly effective; 43 percent believed He would find them respectable, if not wholly successful; while 53 percent said Christ would rate the church as having little positive impact on souls and society" (Colson 1992, 31).

These statistics seem to suggest that, in today's post-modern society, church membership and attendance alone do very little to sway the hearts of men and women toward a greater commitment to God. On the strength of these data, it is natural that Colson's response would be that, "...while plenty of people are still walking through the doors of churches, secularism reigns as the dominant world-view of American culture.... To bring hope to a needy world, the church must be the church" (Colson 1992, 31-32).

I must admit that the phrase, "the church must be the church," sounds like a nice, trendy phrase to throw around at a missions conference. But if we ever were to internalize the concept of the Church as Christ's Body, we would be driven to our knees by our own shame, where we would seek forgiveness from God for having so totally misrepresented Him. Should we ever wonder why we are here and what our mission in the world ought to be, we have but to put our ears to the wind. As we do, we will hear the words of C.S. Lewis, who said,

"...the Church exists for nothing else but to draw men into Christ, to make them little Christs. If they are not doing that, all the cathedrals, clergy, missions, sermons, even the Bible itself, are simply a waste of time. God became man for no other purpose" (Lewis 1943, 155).

And What About the Pentecostals?

This book is not written about Christians or Christianity. It is directed toward those in the Pentecostal community. Whatever indictments might be leveled against the entire Christian Church must also be applied to us, for we are a part of that Body, and therefore, a part of that problem.

An immediate question, then, concerns the state of Modern Pentecostalism. After all, in relation to the rest of Christianity, the Pentecostals are the "new kids on the Christian block," having been around for less than one hundred years. What is our current condition? In comparison with what we might call the *secularized* Christian community, are Pentecostals ready for unlimited hand-to-hand combat against satan and his forces? Again, let's take a peek.

Pentecostalism is now the fastest-growing Christian belief system in the world, increasing at a rate of 19 million new members per year. One out of every five Christians (21%) is Pentecostal. Of the world's four million full-time Christian workers, one million are Pentecostal/Charismatics. Unfortunately, the Pentecostal Movement is represented by 11,000 Pentecostal and 3,000 Charismatic denominations respectively (Burgess, McGee, and Alexander 1988, 810-830). That means that there are as many as 14,000 individual interpretations of what it means to be Pentecostal.

As we refer back to Charles Colson's analysis of American Christianity, the same themes of secularism, self-centeredness, and complacency appear in our evaluation of modern Pentecostalism. Many feel that we have traded in our starry crown in the Kingdom of God, and have exchanged it for a membership card at the country club. One student of the Movement has said, "Let the record show—the greatest threat to a post-modern Pentecostalism is its insatiable love affair with the American ideology" (Adams 1996, 4). Charges like these will lead us either to recoil with resentment or to consider our ways.

I Will Build My Church

I am but one man, and I would not dare attempt to predict the actions of Almighty God. But I am convicted by the Holy Spirit that Jesus is not coming back to this earth to rescue a failing Church. Even before His crucifixion, He announced to God, to satan, and to the rest of the world, "...upon this rock I will build My church; and the gates of hell shall not prevail against it" (Mt. 16:18). The Church may be ailing, but failing she is not! Christ spilled His own blood at

Calvary to win our victory. Too many others have died in defense of His gospel for the Church to die in defeat.

It's really about time—time for us to get serious about our calling, time to make a greater commitment to the cause of Christ. And borrowing directly from Colson's theme, I must add that it's time for Pentecostals to once again become Pentecostal! As we have gazed into the mirror and have looked realistically at our condition, we must borrow words from a song penned by the late inspired songwriter, the Rev. Charles Watkins, that we "Have a long way to go to be like the Lord." How do we respond?

Our hearts must become broken before God in order that He will hear and save us. That must become our number one priority in this hour. And we must heed the words of Leonard Ravenhill, the great English evangelist, who wrote:

> "For this midnight hour, incandescent men are needed. On the day of Pentecost, the flame of the living God became the flame of the human heart to that glorious company. The Church began with these men in the 'upper room' agonizing—and today is ending with men in the supper room organizing. The Church began in revival; we are ending in ritual. We started virile; we are ending sterile. Charter members of the Church were men of heat and no degrees; today many hold degrees, but have no heat! Ah, brethren, flame-hearted men are the crying need of the hour!" (Ravenhill 1959, 157)

Lord Open Our Eyes

In the Book of Second Kings, chapter 6, it is recorded that the Syrian army waged a war against the Israelites. Throughout the conflict, God continued to reveal all of the intended Syrian strategies to Elisha, the Jewish prophet. A frustrated Syrian king thought that there must be a traitor in his camp. Finally, one of his servants informed him that, "Elisha, the prophet that is in Israel, telleth the king of Israel the words that thou speakest in thy bedchamber" (2 Kings 6:12). The Syrian leader sent spies to find Elisha, who, it was determined, was in the city of Dothan.

The Syrian troops arrived in Dothan and surrounded the city, their plan being to capture Elisha and bring him back to their leader. Early the next morning, Elisha's servant got up and went outside, only to discover that the enemy had encompassed them. The frightened man, seeing no means of escape, asked Elisha what their next move ought to be. Elisha responded boldly, "Fear not: for they that be with us are more than they that be with them" (2 Kings 6:16).

Elisha saw beyond the immediate circumstance to what God had provided. A battery of angels was posted just outside the city and was ready to launch an attack in their defense. Knowing this, Elisha prayed, "...Lord...open his [the servant's] eyes, that he may see. And the Lord opened the eyes of the young man; and he saw: and, behold, the mountain was full of horses and chariots of fire round about Elisha" (2 Kings 6:17). God intervened, and all Elisha's company was delivered.

I believe that one of our continuing prayers ought to be, "Lord, open our eyes that we may see what You see." We need to realize that God is our eternal source for protection, for power, for everything. As we walk in greater recognition of who we are in God, our faith, like Elisha's, will increase. In addition, we will begin to realize the manifestation of our potential in God.

Challenge Questions

1. How has the current state of Christianity limited the effectiveness of our witness to the world?
2. What are some of the strategies that the Church of today might employ to regain its position of respectability?
3. How can Pentecostals avoid the institutional pitfalls that have entrapped the larger Christian Movement?
4. In light of the times in which we are living, what should be the top priorities for the Pentecostal Movement during the next few years?

5. In what ways might Pentecostals influence a transformation within the larger Body of Christ in order that it might fufill the purpose God intended for it?

References:

Adams, Michael. "Hope in the Midst of Hart: Torwards a Pentecostal Theology of Suffering." Toronto, Ontario, Canada. A paper presented at the Twenty-fifty Anniversary Meeting of The Society for Pentecostal Studies on March 7-9, 1996.

Barrett, David B. "A Survey of the 20th-Century Pentecostal/Charismatic Renewal in the Holy Spirit, with Its Goal of World Evangelization." Burgess, Stanley M., Gary B. McGee, and Patrick H. Alexander, eds. *Dictionary of Pentecostal and Charismatic Movements*. Grand Rapids, MI: Zondervan Publishing House, 1988.

Burgess, Stanley M., Gary B. McGee, and Patrick H. Alexander, eds. *Dictionary of Pentecostal and Charismatic Movements*. Grand Rapids, MI: Zondervan Publishing House, 1988.

Colson, Charles, and Ellen Santill: Vaugh. *The Body: Being Light in Darkness*. Dallas, London, Vancouver, Melbourne: Word Publishing, 1992.

Lewis, C.S., *Mere Christianity*. New York, NY: Collier Books, Macmillan Publishing Company, 1943.

Ravenhill, Leonard. *Why Revival Tarries*. Minneapolis, MN: Bethany House Publishers, 1959.

Chapter 2

Learning to Walk My Talk

For if any be a hearer of the word, and not a doer, he is like unto a man beholding his natural face in a glass: for he beholdeth himself, and goeth his way, and straightway forgetteth what manner of man he was (James 1:23-24).

Jesus was the visible manifestation of God Himself with unlimited power at His disposal (see Col. 2:9). He was a great teacher and a charismatic leader. He was also a miracle worker. He healed the sick, raised the dead, and turned water into wine. The very wind obeyed His voice. Who among us would not want to perform such feats? But Jesus did not stop there. He was nailed to and died upon a cross at Calvary. He spent three days in a borrowed tomb, then He got up and went into Heaven with complete victory over death, hell, and the grave. All of that is written in plain language that we may see, understand, and believe. It has such a ring of heroism to it. After all, Jesus is the greatest hero that ever lived.

Yes, He was God incarnate. He was certainly a miracle worker, and He still is. It is true that He said and did things like none other before or since. But Jesus, the Son of God and the complete embodiment of God, *willingly* forfeited all of that just to keep His word. That's why, when I think about Jesus, I think, *role model*. He made a commitment to the Father, and to us, and He kept His word. When I study the Scriptures, especially the New Testament, that is the message that jumps out at me.

I have a T-shirt at home with the following inscription on it: *"Walk Your Talk...He did."* Jesus walked His talk. He loved God and

---

He loved people, and He put it into action. He gave it all up for us! Everything that He expects from us, He's already done that and more. That's why I want to serve Him and be like Him.

This book is largely a reflection of what I think about Christ. On one occasion, Jesus asked His disciples, "...whom say ye that I am?" (Mt. 16:15) The apostle Peter's response was, "...Thou art the Christ..." (Mt. 16:16). Today, as Jesus asks us that question individually, my answer to Him is: "Lord, You are the Christ who is alive in me!" I really want to be...like Christ!

Studying God's Word, praying to, worshiping, and praising Him are all valid means through which we may learn about and develop a relationship with God. But personal experience serves as the crucible within which our beliefs are tested and our faith is confirmed. In that regard, I could not claim knowledge of the things said in this text without crediting the experience that has molded me as a person. After all, each of us is a walking statement of his/her own history. In this chapter, I shall highlight some of the key events that have molded my experience and my perspective, both as a man and as a Pentecostal.

Personal Background

I was born on January 25, 1944, in Akron, Ohio, the last of six offspring of Raymond and Ann Robinson. My father was a full-time minister in the Apostolic Pentecostal Movement. My mother was a homemaker and coworker at my dad's church. Throughout my early childhood, the church environment represented the core of my social development. Dad was the pastor (head minister) at two churches, one in Akron and the other in Youngstown, Ohio. As a result, most of my growing-up time was spent immersed in a religious culture.

Growing Up

Although there was great pressure to conform to religious norms, other home training that I received neutralized the possible negative effects of that pressure. Both my parents were college graduates. In addition, all six of the children in my family were required to attend college. Each of us was held to the highest standards of academic and social achievement, and there was no excuse for mediocrity. Rather than just preparing for Heaven, we were also taught to plan and prepare for the future—that is, the future on this earth. My dad emphasized this orientation toward success, not just in our home, but in his congregations as well.

Many times over the years, I saw him stand in the pulpit and recite this phrase: "Good, better, best, never let it rest—until your good gets better and your better gets best." In those days, listening to the minister was considered the same as listening to God. The Pentecostal preacher, so I was taught, was a "spiritually elite" personality who had received a calling from God to proclaim and teach the Bible. Each had been *anointed* by God to understand, interpret, and disseminate God's Word to the masses. In that respect, my dad was no exception. He was my priest and my father, in that order. His words were irrefutable, and he was not to be challenged.

The Ministry of Music

Music was a great source of doctrinal teaching within our culture. I was grounded in my theology by music as much as I was by biblical study. The "gospel song" represented an integral part of our liturgy. The spiritual message in our music was clear enough that anyone hearing it could understand the focus of our beliefs. Songs like, "I'll Fly Away," "Goin' Up Yonder," and "When I Wake Up in Glory By and By," presented the theme that there is a world beyond this one in which we hope to dwell someday. That world, which we call *Heaven*, is up there, beyond the sky. In a time period designated as the "Sweet By and By," we anticipate that we will reside in a land where we will "Never Grow Old." In that land and in that life, we will overcome all the injustices that we have suffered on this earth. Other important themes reflected in Pentecostal music are: the love of God, the sacrifice of Christ, the joy of living for God, and the need to walk by faith.

In addition to the lyrics, the rhythmical style and intensity of gospel music formed a medium through which we expressed both our religious convictions and our Afro-American ethos, or "soul."

My siblings and I sang in the church choir, and we learned to play musical instruments. As a result of that early combination of musical and theological training, I continue to be involved in music ministry today.

Culture Shock

I was well-satisfied with my life as a Pentecostal until I enrolled in college in 1962. During my freshman year at the University of Akron, I encountered Darwin's *Origin of the Species* and consequently experienced my first major "values" conflict. I informed my General Psychology instructor that I rejected the theory of evolution. In response, he suggested that I pay a visit to the campus chaplain. In turn, the chaplain advised that I simply tell the instructor what he wanted to hear, thus ensuring that I would pass the course. I was a Pentecostal. There was no way that I could accept the idea that mankind had evolved from a lower life form. But most of what I knew about religious matters had come through rote learning. I was a classic product of intellectual osmosis, learning to repeat what I had heard from others. This meant that I had no sound theological support for my beliefs.

Unfortunately, when exam time came, I succumbed to the political pressure imposed by the instructor. I passed the course, but something happened inside of me. I felt compromised and violated. It was as though I had helped a robber steal from me. Even though it occurred over 30 years ago, the memory of that event is still fresh. In anger, I decided never to allow political pressure to force me from my beliefs again. In the unfolding of that situation, however, I came to recognize a fundamental weakness in my thinking about spiritual things. I discovered that I knew as little about God as I did about evolution.

A Long Journey Begins

I began to wonder if there were other ideas that I was hearing, both in the church and on the campus, that misrepresented the integrity of God. My dad had painted a picture of God as the One who loved me enough to send His only Son to die for me. There was no way that I wanted to discredit God by remaining ignorant concerning Him. That initial incident in undergraduate school planted a seed of doubt in my mind concerning my knowledge of God. That seed continued to grow, a little at a time, during the rest of my young adult life.

On June 26, 1966, at the age of 21, I married Sylvia Ann Butts. Like me, she was a "P.K." (preacher's kid), steeped in the Pentecostal tradition. Sylvia had a Bible-based mentality. She was familiar with the Scriptures, but more than that, she was also familiar with God. She demonstrated, with a daily practice of faith and trust in God, that the Bible is the Word of God and is meant to be, "...a lamp unto my feet, and a light unto my path" (Ps. 119:105). To this day, I still consider Sylvia my first real Bible teacher.

Although Sylvia's viewpoint and lifestyle fascinated me, it was not particularly relevant to the way I wanted to live at the time. And although I continued to follow the letter of the Pentecostal doctrine for the next 25 years, the spirit of Pentecost, the manifestation of the fullness of life in Christ, failed to permeate my being. Throughout that period, I remained functionally illiterate about the Bible and about God. Without knowing it intellectually, however, my spirit was crying out for a closer walk with Him. That desire motivated me to become a more serious Bible student. Plodding along at first, I eventually reached a basic understanding of some of the principles involved in the Spirit-led life. But studying and praying alone cannot make one holy.

Jesus, on one occasion, confronted a group of religious leaders and scholars. He challenged them, saying, "Search the scriptures; for in them ye think ye have eternal life: and they are they which testify of Me. And ye will not come to Me, that ye might have life" (Jn. 5:39-40). Here, Jesus was clearly describing the gulf that lies in the human mind between the theory and the reality of God's Word. The Pharisees and scribes were studying the Scriptures from a historical and legalistic perspective. Jesus injected Himself into this discourse as the very fulfillment of the writings which they were examining. As far as He was concerned, they were preoccupied with the written Word of God, while not recognizing Him, the *living Word of God.*

Essentially, that was my dilemma as well. I could recite a few Scriptures. I was even a pretty good gospel songwriter. But my fellowship with God was weak and without intimacy. And there was no question that I basically reigned in my own life. For the most part, the following passage penned by Henry David Thoreau represented my motto for daily living: "If a man does not keep pace with his companions, perhaps it is because he hears a different drummer. Let him step to the music he hears, however measured, or far away." I basically walked to the beat of my own drummer, which was fine for me, but certainly not for others.

A Spiritual Double Agent

When I was a kid, Dad would say, "When you don't know something, that's one thing; but when you don't know that you don't know, you're in big trouble." In other words, the worst thing about ignorance is that it does not know. I was certainly ignorant of the fact that I could not manifest the life of God without first living under the authority of God.

Consequently, I became a *spiritual double agent* (aka "hypocrite"), saying one thing and yet living another. In my mind, a little slipping and sliding was okay, as long as no one found out. If I could make it to church on Sunday and if I could stay active in church work, then God would overlook my weaknesses. I believed that He would somehow make everything all right. After all, He was God. Well, He did not make it all right. At least He did not fix things as I thought He would.

A Call and a Promise

In the Fall of 1979, I was working as vice president for operations at the Columbus, Ohio Urban League. I was responsible for coordinating all program services, and I was in training to take over as agency president once my boss moved to our national headquarters in New York. On this particular day, I arrived at my office at about 8:00 a.m. I remember turning on the light and walking across the room to my desk. The Holy Spirit spoke inside me and said, "When you leave this place, I will bless you." I looked around to see who was in the room, knowing that it was too early in the morning for anyone else to be there. Once again, I heard that same simple message: "When you leave this place, I will bless you."

I tried to recall the context within which that idea had entered my mind. I remembered something that I had read in Scripture concerning God's call to Abram. The synopsis of that event is recorded in Genesis chapter 12. God appeared to Abram and told him to leave his father's house and his native country. He led Abram to a strange land and said to him:

> And I will make of thee a great nation, and I will bless thee, and make thy name great; and thou shalt be a blessing: I will bless them that bless thee, and curse him that curseth thee: and in thee shall all families of the earth be blessed. So Abram departed, as the Lord had spoken unto him; and Lot went with him (Genesis 12:2-4).

I was familiar with the general concept of someone being selected by God to do certain things, but I had no idea of the significance of such a calling. During several months afterward, I pondered the words that I had heard in my office. I felt that God must have been telling me to leave the Urban League.

In June, 1980, I resigned my position and started a music production company. This was a difficult task, but I was determined to make it work. The range of services I provided included composing music, producing musical concerts, and offering studio and live recordings.

After two years of toiling and of trying to prove God, it was clear that I was missing the point of what He had been saying. But the question was, "How?" Most of the people for whom I performed services, themselves professing Christians, never paid me. The income that was generated was spent on meeting our basic necessities, so there was nothing left to put back into the business. We had no money to pay bills, including taxes. The Internal Revenue Service imposed a lien against us, and we lost everything, including our home, two automobiles, and other major possessions. With our credit rating completely shattered, all major purchases had to be paid for in cash. I was ignorant of federal bankruptcy laws, so we did not exercise that option either. We still had two of our three children living with us, and we struggled just to have lunch money for them to take to school.

In the midst of this devastation, some wonderful and loving people came to our aid. Both Sylvia's mother and my mother stayed in constant contact with us. Theresa and Walt Stewart often gave us food or took us out to eat. Janet and James Gregory charged us $25.00 for an automobile so that we would not feel too embarrassed at their kindness. For several months, Debbie and Jim Stocks allowed us to stay rent-free in their home. Afterward, we lived with our oldest daughter, Yvonne, in her two-bedroom condominium. Although cramped and terribly inconvenienced, neither Debbie and Jim nor Von ever complained about such an invasion of their privacy.

Eventually, we moved into a small apartment, and I started doing consulting work as well as teaching at a local college. Sylvia went back to work also in order to help restore our financial life. I continued to think about what God had said to me in 1979, knowing that it had made no sense to my family or to me.

Research has shown that issues such as alcoholism, child abuse, and drug addiction affect all members of a family. But understanding God and walking by faith are family issues as well. I was jeopardizing the well-being of my wife and children. My confusion turned into embarrassment and then to resentment toward God. I tried to close that chapter of my life, but it simply was not meant to be.

A Time of Self-Rule

In 1984, I began a new career as a tennis teaching professional. I shared my interest in working in the tennis profession with Albert Matthews, Manager and Head Pro at the Scarborough East Tennis and Fitness Club in Columbus. Al hired me on a part-time basis and then trained me in the basics of teaching tennis. I was given an opportunity to learn and grow and was eventually offered a permanent teaching position at the club. Initially, the long hours reaped a minimal return. Things slowly picked up, however, and I began to experience success. I have been teaching now for 12 years in this challenging profession.

Throughout the 1980's my spiritual development not only stopped, it began to go backward. I did not want to admit it, but I wanted no more to do with God. I was afraid to trust Him, and I felt that He was to blame for my previous failure. During the years 1985 to 1990, tennis became my life, and I was consumed with teaching and playing tournaments. Because of that, there was no time for anyone or anything else. But that was okay, for in the process, I believed that I had shown the world. I had proven to everyone, including God, that I could come back. I felt I had demonstrated my ability to succeed in the power of my own will. To the contrary, I had only proven how self-centered I really was.

Divorce: Like Death Without a Corpse

During the 24 and a half years of our marriage, Sylvia and I raised three beautiful daughters and shared in many wonderful experiences. But our relationship had deteriorated to a point where we seemed to have nothing left. Once this destructive process was set in motion, all the Bible knowledge in the world could not stop it. Numerous times over the years, Sylvia would suggest that we seek professional help to rebuild our crumbling relationship. Often she would say, "Let's pray about it." But I refused to let some outside source (spiritual or human) interfere in our personal life. Instead, at a time when I was completely frustrated and self-protective, I decided to bail out.

On January 22, 1990, Sylvia and I were divorced. On that cold day, the winter wind was especially harsh. There was no hint of sunshine to pierce the morning sky. The cold environment inside the Franklin County Municipal Building rivaled that of the winter outside. Sylvia and I sat in a sterile courtroom, watching as our marriage that had taken half our lives to construct was wiped out in a matter of minutes. I had learned about the sacredness of marriage and how it represents a covenant among two people and God. I was convinced that divorcing Sylvia was the same as divorcing God. So, at that moment I truly believed that my life was destined for eternal destruction. The best way to describe the feeling of that event is to say that, when two people have shared real love, divorce is like dying, but there is no corpse. I can think of no worse failure in my life. In light of this and other blunders, I felt totally disqualified from performing useful service for God. Further, I did not really care.

Other than the outstanding examples previously mentioned, support from family and friends was, for the most part, nonexistent. The deepest hurt of all came from the rejection that Sylvia and I suffered at the hands of the religious community. The church family that we had grown up and worked with for years was now silent and invisible. That response rendered a crushing blow to both of us. We felt completely alienated from our own spiritual heritage. Devastated though we may have been, God had already chosen to involve us in something that, by comparison, made our experience seem like a Sunday school picnic.

A Journey Into Hell

On January 12, ten days before our divorce was final, I was sitting alone in my small studio apartment. I felt like I had died and gone to hell. Overcome with guilt and shame, I was convinced that God was looking down from Heaven and shaking His head in complete disbelief.

In the midst of my own pity party, I received a telephone call from Sylvia stating that one of our friends from church was in the Burn Unit at the Ohio State University (OSU) Hospital. I had met Debbie and Howard Rivers in 1983, having provided the music for their wedding. After that, Sylvia and Debbie developed a close friendship working in the same building and singing in the church choir together. Over the years, we found them to be warm and engaging people. But now, unbelievably, Howard was in the hospital, the victim of an attempted suicide. Debbie called Sylvia and asked if we would come to the hospital to be with her. As soon as I could ready myself, I drove to OSU to meet them. The details of that tragic event were not fully known until much later.

NOTE: Most of the following information concerning the facts of Howard Rivers' attempted suicide has come from interviews that I conducted with Debbie Ruth Rivers, examination of documents that she provided, and from newspaper accounts.

On January 10, 1990, 36-year-old Howard Rivers spent the early evening with his wife, Debbie and their six-year-old son, Bryan. He hugged each of them and said that he had to leave for awhile. But before he left, he composed a letter to Debbie and left it in the basement of their home, lying next to his keys and wallet. A portion of the letter contained these words: "...Remember that I will always love you! Forgive me, Debbie; forgive me, Bryan; forgive me, Lord!" Debbie knew that Howard had been somewhat despondent during the previous weeks, but they had been praying and talking together; and he seemed to be doing okay.

Howard left the house that evening and rode a city bus to Big Run Park located on the west side of Columbus. As the hours passed, Debbie began to worry. She called her father-in-law, but he had not seen or heard from Howard all night. At approximately 4:00 the following morning, Howard, who was still at the park, drank a number of flammable liquids, including brake fluid and anti-freeze. He then poured some of this mixture on his body and ignited himself with a lighter.

Howard's body was now an inferno of flames and peeling flesh. In the midst of this burning hell, Howard cried out to God from the depths of his spirit, "I don't want to be lost!" He ran about 200 yards and came to a house at the edge of the park. Inside, a 64-year-old woman and her husband were sleeping in a first-floor bedroom. Upstairs, a man, who was renting a room in the house, lay sleeping as well—his handgun sitting on a table beside his bed.

Howard picked up a chair from the patio and threw it into the double glass doors at the rear of the house. He then stepped inside and stood at the doorway. The woman, whose husband was recovering from recent heart surgery, got up and went to investigate.

The upstairs tenant awoke hearing the crashing glass. He reported that before going downstairs, he had reached for his gun and then, for no apparent reason, he had inexplicably decided not to take it with him.

Howard, his body in tremendous pain and smoldering, begged the woman, "Get your gun and shoot me, kill me." Instead, she said to him, "No, I'm trying to get you some help." She called 911, telling the dispatcher, "His skin is covered with blood...He's coming back...He's right in my room; he's in my room..." The woman would later tell Debbie that when she saw Howard that morning, she was not aware that he was a black man. She said that his skin was "smoldering like steaks on a grill." Within minutes, several deputy sheriffs arrived. They covered Howard with a sheet and sent him by Life Flight helicopter to OSU Hospital. Although he had incurred third-degree burns over 90 percent of his body, he was able to give the details of his ordeal, telling deputies that he had, in fact, tried to kill himself.

At about 6:00 a.m., the deputies went to the Rivers' home and informed Debbie of what had happened. One of the officers told Debbie that when they had examined the scene of her husband's tragedy, they had found pieces of charred skin on the trees leading up to the house where Howard had sought refuge. Debbie took young Bryan to the day care center, called a close friend, and then proceeded to the hospital to be with Howard. When she arrived, nurses told her that as a result of Howard's condition, he would probably live only a few more hours. As the story was reported via local radio, television, and print media, family and friends began to rally around Debbie. Through her faith and their prayers, she gained strength to discuss Howard's treatment with hospital staff.

"And Fire Cannot Burn the Spirit"

When I arrived at OSU, I rode the elevator up to the Burn Unit. The door opened, and I immediately saw Debbie and Sylvia in the waiting area. As I sat down with them, Debbie turned to me and asked, "Are you ready to go see Howard?" I wanted to say, "No, I am not the one you want." But that was not how God had ordained it. I was not to be let off the hook so easily. Debbie continued, "I want you to pray with him." I'm thinking, *Pray? No, not me!* But before I could come up with an appropriate excuse, she stood up and motioned for me to accompany her to the quarantine area where the burn patients were located.

As we walked down the hallway, I felt useless. My mind was racing, and I thought, *Debbie cannot know what she is doing. I'm not ready! I'm not clean; I'm in the middle of divorcing my wife!* It did not seem fair that I should be asked to pray to a God who probably did not want to hear a word that I had to say. But it was too late for me to back out now.

When we reached the end of the hallway, we entered a small room about eight foot square. In this area we put on gowns and masks in order to protect the patients from germs and possible infection. Inside that cubicle, with no apparent means of escape, I heard the voice of God say to me, "Ask Debbie what she wants for Howard." Here I was again, back at the Urban League in 1979. I knew that voice well. But I knew even more that this was God's business. Suddenly, I was no longer angry with or afraid of Him. Instead, I experienced a deep sense of awe and reverence. Obediently, I asked Debbie what she wanted for Howard and she quickly replied, "I want him to be at peace with God."

We then proceeded into Howard's room where I beheld a sight that I shall never forget. Here was an intelligent and warm husband and father, lying on his back, connected to all kinds of machinery. Howard was wrapped in mummy-like fashion from head to toe. His body was full of morphine so that he was not aware of the physical damage that he had incurred. He was fully conscious as Debbie went over to his bed.

A nurse came in and monitored each of the fluids going into Howard's body. As she left the room, Debbie said to Howard (much too quickly for me), "Brother Bert is here and he is going to pray for you." As Howard looked at me and gave a consenting nod, Debbie grasped my arm and gestured for me to move toward the bed. We closed our eyes, and I began to utter meaningless phrases. The bleakness of the situation made the words sound so empty and irrelevant.

As I stumbled along, feebly searching for something to say, the Holy Spirit, using my voice, spoke a phrase that erupted from inside me like a geyser. He said, "And fire cannot burn the spirit!" Debbie and I froze. We knew instantly that God was speaking. As we listened to the words coming out of my mouth, the environment in the room changed completely. The smell of medicine was transformed into the aroma of Heaven. Everything around us seemed holy! The Holy Spirit continued:

> "This young man called to Me when he was on fire and said that he did not want to be lost. According to My Word, death could not separate him from My love. I heard his cry and reached on the other side of death and saved him. I want all to know that he is now in the hands of a loving God."

When the Holy Spirit finished, Debbie and I stood speechless. We were overcome by what we had just heard. When we opened our eyes, we wept and worshiped God, almost uncontrollably.

Each of us said good-bye to Howard, I for the last time, and we left the room. As we walked back up the hallway to the waiting area, Debbie thanked me for praying with Howard. I took Sylvia back to her house, sharing with her along the way what the Holy Spirit had said. She was stunned also, just as Debbie and I had been, and she was ecstatic about Howard.

"You Will Have to Learn to Walk in That"

When I got back to my apartment, I immediately went before God asking Him about the events of the past two hours. He directed my attention to a particular passage of Scripture. I opened my Bible to Romans chapter 8 and read:

> *For I am persuaded, that neither death, nor life, nor angels, nor principalities, nor powers, nor things present, nor things to come, nor height, nor depth, nor any other creature, shall be able to separate us from the love of God, which is in Christ Jesus our Lord* (Romans 8:38-39).

I closed the Bible and listened once again to the voice of God. He assured me that His love for people is beyond our ability to measure or comprehend. Then, I was stunned again as He spoke these words, "The love that I showed for Howard Rivers is the same love that I have for you. But you will have to learn to walk in that." Since that day, I have not been the same.

I have been asked by some, "If you knew that God was speaking to you and working in your life, how could you proceed to divorce your wife?" I have never found a good theological answer to that question. There is no justification for my decision. The truth is, I did what I wanted to do at the time. I was wrong, and I remain accountable to God for that decision. I have come to realize, however, that it is futile for me to spend the rest of my life trying to correct that mistake, no matter how grave it was. In addition, I am sure that I will make other mistakes before I die. But I am comforted by the fact that I, too, am in the hands of a loving and forgiving God. His Word says, "If we confess our sins, he is faithful and just to forgive us our sins, and to cleanse us from all unrighteousness" (1 Jn. 1:9).

Howard Rivers lived for five more weeks. But before he died, he asked Debbie to go back to church and share with the people the lesson he had learned about the value of knowing Christ. He then said to her, "...and tell Brother Bert thanks for praying with me; I heard every word that he said."

Five years later, Debbie is still attempting to deal with the gravity of that event. Bryan is almost 11 and really needs a father. Until that happens, Debbie is both mother and father to him. She is honest about her continuing pain over the loss of her husband, but she has accepted the fact that God has allowed that to be part of her experience on this earth. Debbie has developed a keen awareness of the sustaining power of God. Since Howard has been gone, she has had to depend on God for everything. In the continuing course of her recovery, she entertains thoughts of falling in love again and perhaps of remarrying. I pray that for her, as well.

When I asked Debbie's permission to use the foregoing account as part of this text, she readily consented, adding her hope

)ne hearing this story will be motivated toward God. If no one else is encouraged, I am. *"Thank you, Debbie and Howard!"*

Individuality Versus Individualism

Each of us is created as a unique specimen of God's imagination. We possess internal and external attributes that make us different from one another. King David said, "I will praise thee; for I am fearfully and wonderfully made: marvellous are Thy works; and that my soul knoweth right well" (Ps. 139:14). But our individuality and uniqueness do not preclude our responsibility to God. He issues a requirement for every person, "...to fear the Lord thy God, to walk in all His ways, and to love Him, and to serve the Lord thy God with all thy heart and with all thy soul" (Deut. 10:12).

In 1979, I heard God say to me, "When you leave this place, I will bless you." Because I had not known the true meaning of those words at that time, I had misrepresented God's purpose in my life. The lingering agony of that experience caused me to close the door on God's work of perfection in me. But even as I chose to walk to the "beat of a different drummer," God was gracious and faithful, trusting, of course, in His own integrity. In addition, He trusted in me. He knew the exact day and time when I would return to Him. And He knew that I would ask that He show Himself to me and reign in me.

Until 1996, some questions yet remained: What place did God want me to leave? Why was a blessing promised, but pain and disappointment followed? And why was there so much loss? I know that I have been created a unique individual. I have been imprinted with specific traits of character and personality. I have been equipped with strengths and weaknesses for the purpose of showing forth the glory of God as He has established it in me. His promise at that time was, "...and I will bless you." In other words, *He* would be the source of blessing, not me.

God was asking me to leave that place of independence from Him, and nothing less would be acceptable. No place or condition renders us more useless to God's purpose than individualism. In the Kingdom of God, individualism is seen as a spirit. It manifests itself as an attitude of faith in one's self, rather than of faith in God. He wants us to be proud of being His creation. But He holds us accountable to let go of our right to operate independently from Him. God expects us to dethrone our own self-will and willingly enthrone Him. Let me elaborate.

Abraham's Example

I do not pretend to put myself on the same level with Abraham. He represents an example, however, of the principle that God is teaching here. Abram, as he was first known, was 75 years old when God called him and promised that all the nations of the earth would be blessed through his seed. Abram was anxious to help the process along. Therefore, he and his wife, Sarai, decided that, because she was too old to bear children (she was 65), Abram should conceive a son through Hagar, one of Sarai's young handmaids. Eleven years later, when Abram was 86 years old, Hagar bore Ishmael. God assured them that although Ishmael would be blessed, he was not the seed that God had ordained in His promise. Ishmael would not be the heir to Abram's throne.

Thirteen years later, when Abram was 99, God entered into a covenant with him. Abram's name was changed to "Abraham," and Sarai's to "Sarah." In the covenant, God promised that they would conceive a son and that they would name him "Isaac." One year later, 91-year-old Sarah bore Isaac, the promised son. The nation of Israel, therefore, appeared through the lineage of Isaac, not of Ishmael.

The Lesson

It does not take a Bible scholar to understand that Ishmael was a product of the natural will of Abram, and Isaac was the child of Abraham's faith. During our lifetime, we will each have an "Ishmael"; we will produce something from our own desire and self-will. It may be a career move or a financial decision. It may even be something that we consider unimportant. Whatever the nature of it, an eternal effect will be rendered. We can be certain that if it is born of our will and not of the will of God, it will return to haunt us. God will reveal the nature of the thing in the light of His purpose, and we will be asked to trade it in for that which He calls *best*.

This is a lesson that is born from experience alone. It is too crucial to be learned in any other way. Some people learn it during an earlier part of their life, but others come to it much later. This one thing is certain: When God establishes His purpose in us, He does not spend time wondering if we will ever respond. He only concerns Himself with *when* we will respond.

Howard Rivers and I both had to learn that God will not tolerate those who live independently from Him. We each faced the reality of coming to the end of our self-will and individualism and then being loved back into the heart of God. I did not realize it at the time, but at the very moment that I was praying for Howard, God was praying for me. Howard's discovery was made when he was 36 years old. He never got the opportunity to leave the hospital in order to tell his part of the story. Five weeks after I saw him, he died. As a result of God's mercy and grace, I am alive today so that I may speak for both of us.

Sylvia has granted me forgiveness, and though the pain of our loss remains, we are trusting that God will grant us comfort and guidance. On the other hand, most of our Christian friends and associates are still nowhere to be found. Perhaps their need to judge outweighs their ability to forgive. This is certainly not mentioned in a spirit of accusation, but in the hope that we will all learn better how to love. God, the one most offended by my mistakes, has granted me the biggest reprieve. I am grateful that I was not destroyed. In my gratitude, I share the sentiments of the apostle Paul, who said:

> *Brethren, I count not myself to have apprehended: but this one thing I do, forgetting those things which are behind, and reaching forth unto those things which are before, I press toward the mark for the prize of the high calling of God in Christ Jesus* (Philippians 3:13-14).

The Jew and the Pentecostal

On July 30,1994, I married Deborah Schiff Wilburn. She has experienced the sting of divorce as well, but she maintains a high sense of integrity and pride. Debbie lives daily with the attitude that the future holds promise to those who keep going.

Marriage between a Jew and a Pentecostal is a rather unlikely occurrence. This notwithstanding, our experience is reaping a fruitful harvest of mutual understanding and support. We share a common interest in important areas of life (i.e. reverence for God, family values, interest in educational advancement, "tennis junkies," and an excitement about being alive). We further believe that we are part of a larger plan in the heart of God.

Debbie's cultural background has established within her a passion for family. A day does not pass that she is not planning some special activity for her two sons, Daniel and Brian, who are ages 15 and 13 respectively. For Debbie, worship is not concluded with a public display that takes place inside a building. In fact, it is not public at all. Worship for her is the attitude and act of accepting the responsibility that accompanies one's God-given authority.

Debbie's work ethic is summed up best in the three words from the Nike commercials: "Just do it!" She has done it for a long time. In March, 1993, Debbie earned her Ph.D. in Foreign Language Education from the Ohio State University. She is actively involved in her profession, serving as assistant professor, researcher, writer, and private consultant. Additionally, among her numerous other duties, Debbie has become involved in the development of this text. I have officially named her my "editor-in-chief." More than that, I love her deeply, and she is my friend.

"...The Desert Shall Rejoice, and Blossom as the Rose."

Jesus said, "I am the vine, ye are the branches: He that abideth in Me, and I in him, the same bringeth forth much fruit: *for without Me ye can do nothing*" (Jn. 15:5). As much as we might not want to admit it, we all need God and we cannot escape His dealings in our lives. What began for me in college in 1962 as an attempt to resolve a question on creation theory, developed into a long journey of personal development and growth in God. In this dynamic, life-changing process, I have found that God does not require us to attain perfection in the power of our own will, for He knows that we are incapable of reaching that goal alone. Instead, He desires that we live in an attitude wherein we trust in Him and submit to His will, knowing that He is perfecting us every day.

God has spoken profoundly about His willingness to redeem and to restore us. Through the prophet Isaiah, He has said, "The wilderness and the solitary place shall be glad for them; and the desert shall rejoice, and blossom as the rose" (Is. 35:1). Paradoxically, and in the midst of my own personal hell, God has resurrected my life. He has lifted me beyond the guilt and loss and has given me comfort and strength. Out of the ashes of failure and brokenness, my dreams have reappeared, and this writing has become a reality. In retrospect, I can look back and see how God has been shaping my life from the beginning. I am grateful that He has given me time to listen to His voice and to see His handiwork. I know that He is not through with me yet. And wherever He is guiding me, I am confident that He knows the best way to be glorified in me.

Conclusion

Sometimes when we think that we have gone out of bounds from God and that He can no longer retrieve us, we are about to be surprised. For, at a moment when we least expect it, God will invade our hearts with His love, and we will begin to walk in the power of the resurrected life. Isaiah explained it this way: "And the parched ground shall become a pool, and the thirsty land springs of water: in the habitation of dragons, where each lay, shall be grass with reeds and rushes" (Is. 35:7).

God has been gracious to me, and I shall forever be indebted to Him. But I have learned, perhaps the hard way, that the issue of personal commitment and accountability is a serious matter. I would rather have made the discovery about the goodness and mercy of God without having inflicted so much pain on the people who were closest to me. Those types of memories are slow to disappear. Finally, I am just now beginning to understand what it really means to "walk my talk."

Challenge Questions:

1. In what ways might practical experience serve to alter or confirm one's religious beliefs?
2. Is it appropriate for us to question traditionally held beliefs, or is this against the will of God?
3. What is our responsibility in resolving contradictions between our own values and those of the popular culture?
4. What is the Church's role in helping people to address practical survival issues?
5. Should we expect God to be involved in our everyday living or is He concerned only with our spiritual development?

References:

The Columbus Dispatch. Columbus, OH: January 12, 1990, p. 1B.

Rivers, Debbie Ruth. Columbus, OH: personal interviews conducted during the summer of 1995.

Chapter 3

An Assignment From the Father

Then the Lord put forth His hand, and touched my mouth. And the Lord said unto me, Behold, I have put My words in thy mouth (Jeremiah 1:9).

Called and Chosen, but Unprepared

I first thought about writing this book in the latter part of 1991, convinced that the vision, the original motivation of it, was God-given. As I first sat down to write, it seemed a simple matter of transcribing the sacred words that God would dictate. I had read how He used Moses to write the Ten Commandments in this way. In fact, I thought every word in the Bible had originated from the mouth of God and the so-called biblical authors were actually *spiritual secretaries.*

Something went wrong. Either someone was stealing God's words out of the sky before they reached me, or I simply was not prepared to perform such a serious endeavor. Although the latter was obviously true, I learned a great lesson. In the process of my floundering, I discovered that God's expectation of me did not stop when I was chosen to write this book. He was holding me accountable to perform at a high standard and to meet the prerequisite requirement of preparing myself for the task. Additionally, I learned that God was patient and that He was willing to work through me, at my pace, in order to fulfill this mission.

I set aside the task of writing in favor of a return to the proverbial "drawing board." In September, 1992, I began an 18-month process of consecration and disciplined study of God's Word and other pertinent material. During the first nine months, I attended the World Harvest Bible College. In an environment that combined faith and disciplined academic pursuit, I was able to focus my attention on gaining an understanding of *Bible basics*. Five days each week, classes convened between 7:30 a.m. and noon. In the afternoons and evenings I worked at my regular job, teaching tennis at the Scarborough East Tennis Club. During that period, much time was spent alone with God. Something within me had created an insatiable desire to know more about Him, and I did not want this unique opportunity to pass.

When that first basic-training phase had ended, I spent the next several months carefully researching my own theological and personal belief system. I entered that process thinking that I was one of the only ones engaged in such a process. I soon realized just how wrong I was. The Holy Spirit guided me to a rich reservoir of material and to an international pool of experts in the field of Pentecostal studies.

I have since become affiliated with the Society for Pentecostal Studies and have enjoyed fruitful and exciting fellowship with an expanded fraternity of believers. It is reassuring to know that God wants us to succeed in our endeavors. But it is also amazing how He ordains and endorses our steps as we: (1) dedicate ourselves to the fulfillment of His purpose; (2) remain sensitive within our spirits to the things that are going on around and within us; (3) take our own journey one step at a time; and (4) are willing to do some work.

By September, 1994, I was ready to write again. This time, instead of waiting on God to *dictate* what I should say, I chose the title and subject matter for this text and sought His guidance in formulating the ideas that He had inspired. Unable to type, I took a word processing course at a local community college. Because I had already developed the habit of spending the morning hours in study, I simply devoted that same time to writing. I am proud of the product of my labor. But more than that, I am appreciative of the sacredness of that time—time spent in the presence of Almighty God.

Educational and Professional Background

My academic and professional background provided another element of preparation. In 1967, I earned a B.A. degree in Sociology from the University of Akron (Akron, Ohio). In 1975, I received an M.S. degree in Social Administration from Case Western Reserve University (Cleveland, Ohio). My areas of concentration were Social Planning and Social Research.

I spent 15 years in the social work profession, working in the areas of juvenile justice, community services planning and fund raising, neighborhood community organization, and substance abuse intervention. I completed my social work tenure by serving as vice president for Operations at the Columbus (Ohio) Urban League. I lectured in the social sciences at the University of Akron and at Otterbein College and Columbus State Community College in Columbus, Ohio. I also owned and operated New Song, Inc., a company that specialized in the production and recording of sacred music.

I have been involved in private consulting and training in the areas of social research, community planning, social program evaluation, grant writing, human relations, and church corporate development throughout Ohio and other parts of the Midwest. As previously mentioned, I am certified as a tennis teaching professional by the United States Professional Tennis Association (USPTA) and have been engaged in that profession for the past 12 years. I continue to be involved in private consulting in the area of church organizational development, planning, and management.

Objectivity and Faith

The above training and experience have given me a disciplined foundation within a variety of settings. But my earlier theological roots, those of the apostolic Pentecostal tradition, had produced a skepticism within me about applying these abilities to the religious sphere. I was somewhat hesitant to approach sacred matters through objective examination because I felt that faith and objectivity were in opposition to each other. I was like many others in my generation who thought that if knowledge could be arrived at through empirical (quantifiable) study, then it was not a product of faith. Hence, if it were not of faith, then it could not be of God.

God has helped me to resolve this conflict so that I can now bring the full range of my knowledge and experience into my ministry. In addition to pure consecration, objective pursuit appears to be an essential ingredient for gaining access into the heart of God. There are several reasons for my belief in this regard.

First, objective examination of the things of God helps to build our faith because it allows God to confirm Himself to us. Charles Colson offers the following:

> "All meaning and understanding are rooted in the ultimate reality of the God who is. Apart from Him, nothing was created. Apart from Him, we are unable to perceive or to deduce truth about anything...Ultimate reality embodied in God and Christ is the most consistent theme in Scripture" (Colson 1992, 152-153).

In other words, any proposition that is not built upon the foundation of God as the standard for all truth is invalid.

Second, objectivity forces us to lay aside our predispositions and prejudices so that we may simply ask God to teach us His ways. Solomon said, "Trust in the Lord with all thine heart; and lean not unto thine own understanding. In all thy ways acknowledge Him, and He shall direct thy paths" (Prov. 3:5-6). The more that God is confirmed in us, the more valid our witness of Him will be. A challenge for us then, is to learn the nature and character of God as He is revealed in Christ.

A third value in the objective study of God is that it helps to clarify the direction that our lives will take. It is in the process of our pursuit in God that we can expect to discover His will. Faithful investigation of spiritual things places us in the hands of the Holy Spirit, who teaches us about the orderly fashion of God's operation, including the specific ways in which He intervenes in our lives in order that His will might be performed in us.

For We Walk by Faith...

God cannot be comprehended through objective processing alone. We may exhibit the truth of His character only through the practice of our faith. And that faith must be alive within our hearts and minds. We may conclude, therefore, that our natural faculties of reason and deliberation are useful in spiritual matters only to the extent that they help us to discern the true Spirit of God. When we approach God, we must approach Him by faith. For, as we have clearly heard, "...the just shall live by his faith" (Hab. 2:4).

God is real. He is not a figment of our imagination. He does not need our mental assent in order to operate as God. He is objective, yet our religious thoughts are subjective. He is factual; our perceptions of Him are approximate. Therefore, we must always be willing to test our fervent convictions against the truth of God's Word.

Through disciplined study and consecration, we become better equipped to passionately express the truth that God reveals to us. This truth becomes a gyroscope for life, enabling us to stay centered in God's will. I like the phrase that says, "Show me a man who will stand for nothing and I will show you a man who will fall for anything." Where there is no conviction, there will be no witness.

What I Bring to This Task

Although I have developed certain skills in analyzing social and behavioral phenomena, that alone is not what qualifies me for this assignment. I am neither a scientist nor a theologian. Instead, what makes me the most suited for the present task is that it is of the Lord's choosing. Having inward peace concerning that fact has helped me to stay focused on my responsibility. Moreover, I bring to this process three major strengths: I am a disciplined learner, an informed believer, and a willing servant. Allow me to explain.

1. I am a *disciplined student and learner of God*. Whatever God has for me, I am willing to follow after, that I may know Him. "Study to show thyself approved unto God, a workman that needeth not to be ashamed, rightly dividing the word of truth" (2 Tim. 2:15). Studying God goes way beyond studying the Bible. As Ruler of all the universe, He is at work in the sustaining process of His creation all the time. God must be observed, therefore, in the context of His total operation rather than just as we see Him in the pages of the Holy

It is my desire to see His handiwork and yield to His fi-ty in all matters of life.

The Bible must remain the primary instrument with which we confirm our observations about God. As we filter all revelation through the microscope of His anointed Word, we learn daily of His divine purpose. We are under the tutoring of the Holy Spirit, who will define precisely what is being shown to us from the library of Heaven. Note the words of Paul the apostle:

Now we have received, not the spirit of the world, but the spirit which is of God; that we might know the things that are freely given to us of God. Which things also we speak, not in the words which man's wisdom teacheth, but which the Holy Ghost teacheth; comparing spiritual things with spiritual (1 Corinthians 2:12-13).

The more I examine God and His Word, the more I am examined and changed. The more I learn about spiritual things, the more carnal I realize I am. Conversely, the light of God's glory will be reflected in me to the degree that I am submissive to His will.

2. I am an *informed believer* in the things of God and of Christ. I have said before that I am no religious expert. On the other hand, to the best of my knowledge, I trust nothing about God that is not true.

As we seek God through disciplined study, He constantly teaches us and exposes us to His truth. In addition, God confirms Himself through His mighty acts. God is comprehensive and complex. And yet, all His bidding is motivated by a simple love for us that has no measure or precondition. And it is a love that never ends. I have heard about God from others. Moreover, I have read and studied a great deal about His identity, His ability, and His plan for mankind. I have seen examples of His interventions in the affairs of men. But my most intimate knowledge of God has come from learning how He is working in me.

3. I am a *servant of God.* I have never been crushed by the hand of God; therefore, I do not serve Him out of fear of reprisal. I do not share the experience of those who say that God forced them

into obedience. Although that may be true for them, my passion for God has developed through a different process. I responded to God when He took my breath away by showering me with His unconditional love. My testimony is expressed in the words of the prophet Jeremiah, who said,

> *It is of the Lord's mercies that we are not consumed, because His compassions fail not. They are new every morning: great is Thy faithfulness. The Lord is my portion, saith my soul; therefore will I hope in Him* (Lamentations 3:22-24).

God's ultimate purpose in our learning is not that we become more *informed*, but that we become *transformed* into the image of the living Christ. Under the Old Covenant, God told Habbakuk, "...Write the vision, and make it plain upon tables, that he may run that readeth it" (Hab. 2:2). When we are convinced of God's Word, we will also be convicted by it. And we will be changed!

When Saul of Tarsus, the learned Jewish scholar and zealot, was stunned by the ecstatic revelation of Christ, he could only respond in one way. Blinded by the glory of God and lying prostrate on the ground, he asked, "Lord, what wilt thou have me to do?" (Acts 9:6) My desire is to stay focused on completing the will of God in my life. I am learning to trust Him more each day, and I believe that He trusts me.

The Role of Pentecostal Scholarship

One of God's gifts to us, in our efforts to gain a better understanding of the past and the present and to plot a course for the future of the Pentecostal Movement, has been the introduction of a new breed of disciplined scholars. This is not to diminish or challenge in any way the significance of Spirit-led pastors, evangelists, prophets, teachers, ministers, missionaries, and other Christian workers. But it seems to me that we have come to a point in our development where we need to examine ourselves in the light of our purpose within God's *master plan for the Church*. In that regard, we need all the help we can get.

Although some scholarship has existed within the Pentecostal Movement since its beginning, the level of formalized academic study among Pentecostal and non-Pentecostal scholars has risen dramatically over the past 25 years. An example of that trend has been the formation of the Society for Pentecostal Studies, founded in November, 1970.

Established under the initial leadership of William Menzies, Vinson Synan, and Horace Ward (Burgess, McGee, and Alexander 1988, 793), the Society exists as an international organization of scholars working within the Pentecostal and Charismatic traditions. In its attempt to stimulate discussion regarding various Pentecostal and Charismatic-related issues, the Society sponsors an annual research conference and publishes *PNEUMA: The Journal of the Society for Pentecostal Studies.*

One of the most comprehensive written works concerning the Pentecostal and Charismatic heritage is the *Dictionary of Pentecostal and Charismatic Movements* (Zondervan Publishing House). In print since 1988, this document is replete with information concerning many historical, theological, sociological, and biographical aspects of the Pentecostal Movement.

Current space will not allow an exhaustive listing of the growing volumes of Pentecostal-related literature. I will say, however, that the availability of such material allows for further discussion and clarification of Pentecostal and Charismatic ideals. This discourse also exposes Pentecostals to a wider and more diverse audience, thus enhancing the continued end-time spread of the gospel.

Conclusion

This chapter has focused upon the combined process of disciplined scholarship and consecration that has guided the development of this text. Human beings have been outfitted with the potential to be and to do all that God has ordained for us spiritually. And although God is totally capable of fulfilling that goal in us, we must be willing to submit to His dealings in order that His glory be made manifest through us on the earth.

Disciplined and objective pursuit is a foundational requirement for learning about God. We cannot accurately follow Him through our feelings and thoughts alone. But biblical study and analysis is not a one-way street, for while we are studying God, He is examining us through the standard of His Word. Therefore, whatever calling or assignment we accept from God will be accompanied by a challenge to become spiritually equipped to perform it.

The process of God's perfection in us will not be completed during our lifetime. For as long as we pursue this earthly existence, God will persist in asking more from us than we think is appropriate to give. But with the asking, we are given His promise that, "...He which hath begun a good work in you will perform it until the day of Jesus Christ" (Phil. 1:6).

Challenge Questions

1. Should there be a balance between faith and reason, or are the two mortal enemies?
2. What value might there be in examining one's religious beliefs against traditional orthodox views?
3. What strategies might be useful in attempting to resolve one's theological beliefs with real life?
4. Why is consecration devoid of scholarship an inadequate means of attaining an effective relationship with God?
5. Conversely, can experience be an effective substitute for consecration and disciplined study (in the spiritual arena)?

References:

Burgess, Stanley M., Gary B. McGee, and Patrick H. Alexander, eds. *Dictionary of Pentecostal and Charismatic Movements.* Grand Rapids, MI: Zondervan Publishing House, 1988.

Colson, Charles, and Ellen Santilli Vaughn. *The Body: Being Light in Darkness*. Dallas, London, Vancouver, Melbourne: Word Publishing, 1992.

Part 2

Understanding the Pentecostal Perspective

And there appeared unto them cloven tongues like as of fire, and it sat upon each of them. And they were all filled with the Holy Ghost, and began to speak with other tongues, as the Spirit gave them utterance (Acts 2:3-4).

Chapter 4

"What Meaneth This?"

But ye shall receive power, after that the Holy Ghost is come upon you: and ye shall be witnesses unto me both in Jerusalem, and in all Judea, and in Samaria, and unto the uttermost part of the earth (Acts 1:8).

Determining the Pentecostal Mandate

Jesus proclaimed that the outpouring of the Holy Spirit would reap a worldwide harvest of souls for the Kingdom of God. Within a few days of that statement, the Christian Church was born. On the Day of Pentecost, multitudes watched in amazement as 120 believers began praising and magnifying God in a variety of languages under the inspiration of the Holy Spirit. The onlookers, wondering about the significance of this event, asked the question, "What meaneth this?" (Acts 2:12b) Peter stood and proclaimed that God was doing a new thing among His people. Revival had come, not only to the city of Jerusalem, but to the world! And the rest is history.

Today, as the Pentecostal phenomenon continues to spread throughout the earth, the question is still being asked: "What does this mean?" A growing number of persons both from within and without the Church want to know what Modern Pentecostalism is and what is unique about its claims. These are critical questions, not just for the survival of the current movement, but for the final generation of Pentecostals as well. As the world-evangelistic campaign progresses, our participatory function is in question. Pentecostal leaders are fundamentally concerned about how to promote the movement as a relevant model for life in a post-industrial society.

It is my contention that Pentecostals have always had an assigned role to play in God's *"Master Plan for the Redemption of Humankind."* In that regard, I propose that His threefold "mandate for Pentecostalism" in this century was:

1. To recapture the spirit of God's redemptive vision as established under the Old Covenant and fulfilled in the New Covenant;
2. To restore to the Christian Church the full complement of power, faith, and activity begun on the Day of Pentecost and continued throughout the first century; and
3. To help prepare the Church for the return of Christ.

I believe that it is important to determine if this position is valid and, if so, whether or not it is being pursued. If we have fallen short in any area, is there a chance for us to recover some of our former glory? Our forward vision must include a necessary backward glance.

This chapter begins a four-part analysis of the state of the Modern Pentecostal Movement. Our immediate task is to trace the development of the movement in order to better understand its current nature and character.

The Birth of Modern Pentecostalism

On January 1, 1901, a group of students at a Bible School in Topeka, Kansas sought to experience a new dimension of God's power. As they waited prayerfully, the Holy Spirit descended upon them as He had on the Day of Pentecost (see Acts 2:4), and from that humble beginning, the Modern Pentecostal Movement was born.

As soon as the Pentecostal newborns came out of the womb, they started trying to run. They were convinced that they had been born into the world of the "end time" and that Jesus was about to crack the eastern skies. Therefore, they never took the time to be infants. They did not allow themselves the necessary time to suckle from the breast of God's anointed teaching. Hence, they never developed a clear picture of God's real purpose for them.

Instead of crawling first, as most infants do, they stood right away upon weak legs of incomplete scriptural understanding and tried to run as fast as possible. Because they were not sure where they were running, they heaped upon themselves layer after layer of hastily contrived and often conflicting doctrines. The result was a theological maze that was difficult to navigate in the real world. And since they never went outside to play with the other infants and children of that day, they did not learn how to interact properly with those who were different from themselves.

The early Pentecostals were soon rejected by the religious establishment and that became more than they could bear. Therefore, Pentecostals sought acceptance among the very people who had defined them as religious hacks. In their efforts to join the fraternity of respectable Christianity, they began to let down their guard and some of their standards as well. During the past few years, the doctrinal, political, and social pendulum has swung terribly far in the other direction.

We, who are currently in the movement, have had to grow up fast and yet, in some ways, we have not really grown up at all. An identity crisis has left us reeling and we are currently trying to regain our balance. Dr. Cheryl Bridges Johns, in a rather diagnostic tone, offers that Modern Pentecostalism, "...stands at a crossroads between life or stagnation, between maturity or neurosis and between a diffused identity and a unified core" (Bridges Johns 1995, 4). In other words, we are no longer certain who we are, what we believe, or where we are going. In our wandering state, we are left to cry from the depths of our wounded souls, asking our Great Physician to come and heal us. And He has already promised that, "The Lord is nigh unto them that are of a broken heart; and saveth such as be of a contrite spirit" (Ps. 34:18).

Most students of the movement believe that the absence of a clear and common Pentecostal identity is the root challenge for our future development. As we try to get back on track, we must reformulate our ideology, clarify our mission, and develop strategies for our continued existence. It is my desire to assist, even if in a small way, in the process of our recovery.

Identifying Pentecostals

Specifying those groups and individuals who are Pentecostal in experience and in self-description is a task that is not so easily accomplished. In fact, as the next few pages will demonstrate, it is impossible to limit Pentecostalism to a homogeneous grouping of believers. We can, however, trace the fundamental themes that are common to those who have celebrated the "Feast of Pentecost" during this century.

The Pentecostal Movement is divided among three versions or "waves" of development: Classical Pentecostalism, the Charismatic Movement, and the Non-Pentecostal/non-Charismatic, mainstream church renewal. Together, they comprise one-fifth (21 percent) of all Christian church members (Burgess, McGee, and Alexander 1988, 810-811). Kilian McDonnell says that in 1990, the total number of Pentecostal adherents (all three waves) was 372 million worldwide (McDonnell 1995, 165). But let us delineate the three groups somewhat further.

Classical Pentecostals (first wave) are Spirit-filled Christians who are members of explicitly Pentecostal denominations. Comprising slightly more than half of all Pentecostals (52 percent), membership is primarily based upon receiving the baptism in the Holy Spirit and speaking in other tongues as the Spirit gives the utterance. Additional spiritual gifts, such as prophecy, divine healing, and others, may also accompany Spirit baptism. The standard historical view places the beginning of Classical Pentecostalism at 1901, though some strains of the movement appeared as early as 1741 (Burgess, McGee, and Alexander 1988, 810).

The Charismatic Renewal (second wave), popularized in the 1950's and 1960's, is primarily made up of those who have received Holy Spirit baptism as prescribed above, but who have remained with their own mainline denominations. They make up 38 percent of the movement and include those of the Catholic Renewal.

The third wave of the Pentecostal Movement is known as the non-Pentecostal, non-Charismatic, mainstream church renewal. Appearing in the 1970's and 1980's, this group consists of Evangelical and other Christians who have recently become energized by, though not necessarily filled with, the Holy Spirit. They have, for the most part, remained with their mainline Christian denominations. The early part of this time period witnessed the birth of Messianic Judaism, representing the first distinctively Jewish form of Christianity.

The third-wavers do not recognize a baptism in the Holy Spirit separate from conversion, and they tend to see tongues as optional and unnecessary. Although they represent 14 percent of the statistical Pentecostal numbers, third-wavers do not generally identify themselves with either Pentecostals or Charismatics.

The following data demonstrates that the Pentecostal Movement represents a broad-ranged demographic spectrum (Burgess, McGee, and Alexander 1988, 811):

- 71 percent of Pentecostals worldwide are non-white; 29 percent are white;
- There are more females than males, with children (under 18) outnumbering adults;
- 66 percent of Pentecostals live in the Third World and 32 percent live in the West;
- 87 percent of Pentecostals live in poverty; 13 percent are affluent;
- More Pentecostals tend to be members of a family; and
- Pentecostalism is increasing at a rate of 19 million new members a year.

Although North American Pentecostalism represents but one-third of the movement's total membership, most of my analytical comments will be addressed to that segment of the Pentecostal population. That is because it is the arena of my own knowledge and experience.

Pentecostalism Defined

The above description of the Pentecostal community seems to be rather broad, allowing for an elastic interpretation of Pentecostal ethics. When defined, however, the term *Pentecostalism* takes on a somewhat narrower meaning. William Menzies, Assemblies of God historian, says that:

> "The Pentecostal Movement is that group of sects within the Christian Church which is characterized by the belief that the occurrence mentioned in Acts chapter 2 on the Day of Pentecost not only signaled the birth of the church, but described an experience available to believers in all ages. The experience of an enduement with power, called the 'baptism in the Holy Spirit,' is believed to be evidenced by the accompanying sign of speaking with other tongues as the spirit gives utterance" (Menzies 1971, 9).

Although this statement seems to be rather stringent, it implies that:

- Pentecostalism is a sect (hence, a part) of Christianity;
- "Believer" identifies one who has believed in and confessed the lordship of Christ and is, therefore, already saved. In the above definition, a *believer* is eligible to receive Spirit baptism;
- Christians, like Pentecostals, are saved by the sinless blood of Christ, but unlike Pentecostals, they are not necessarily Spirit-filled;
- Because Spirit baptism is an additional grace offered by Christ to the believer (one who is already saved), then it cannot be considered as a prerequisite to salvation; and
- Spirit baptism, including the speaking in tongues, was a normal experience for believers on the Day of Pentecost and, therefore, it should be normal and expected by them today.

Donald Dayton suggests that Menzies' definition, "...captures the key claim of Pentecostalism and indicates why it carries the name that it does" (Dayton 1987, 24). This "key claim" to which Dayton refers is that of the baptism in the Holy Spirit as a Bible-based experience that is available to anyone who desires to receive it.

It has already been noted that Pentecostalism is not a monolithic or single-minded tradition. According to Faupel and others, there are three primary variations to the definition of Pentecostal-ism as offered above:

1. Those teaching a doctrine of sanctification in the Wesleyan Holiness tradition (the "three works of grace"—Pentecostals who maintain that Christian experience normally finds expression in a pattern of conversion, "entire sanctification," as a distinct subsequent experience, and a further baptism in the Holy Spirit empowering the believer for witness and service, evidenced by speaking in tongues);

2. Those reducing this pattern to "two works of grace" by collapsing the first two into one "finished work" supplemented by a process of gradual sanctification (thus advocating a pattern focusing on conversion and a subsequent baptism in the Holy Spirit as just defined); and

3. Those holding a "Oneness" or "Jesus Only" view of the Godhead (thus proclaiming an "Evangelical unitarianism" of the Second Person of the Trinity) (Dayton 1987, 18).

Although there is this diversity of application, most Pentecostals agree that the baptism in the Holy Spirit, with tongues as the sign of initial evidence, is the center piece of the Pentecostal ideal.

Those who are baptized in the Holy Spirit, and who speak in tongues under the Spirit's influence, interpret it as a reenactment of the initial outpouring of the Holy Spirit on the Day of Pentecost (see Acts 2: 1-4) and cited several other times throughout the Book of Acts (8:4-19; 9:1-19; 10:44-48; 11:15-17; 19:1-7). Although most Pentecostals cannot explain with exactness the nature of the change that has occurred within their hearts and minds, they are unanimous in their testimony that they have been infused with the very life of God. But beyond the experience of Spirit baptism, what is it that Pentecostals believe?

Pentecostal Doctrine

Pentecostalism is, first and foremost, a *movement of the Spirit.* Pentecostals believe that the Holy Spirit has come to breathe the life of Christ into the Church and to thrust each believer into a new

Christ-centered culture. Holy Spirit baptism brings about a complete internal transformation in which the believer becomes, "...a new creature: old things are passed away; behold, all things are become new" (2 Cor. 5:17).

Pentecostals are convinced that the Bible is the "Word" of God, having been literally breathed out, inspired, and ordained by Him. Because the Scriptures represent the standard for all belief and doctrine, Pentecostal claims are traceable to a logic within the biblical text. With roots growing out of the ground of the first-century Church, Pentecostals see themselves as *living out of the Bible*. It is here that we see an important role of the Holy Spirit, that of providing an accurate revelation of Scripture.

Pentecostals read the Bible through the "eyes" of the Holy Spirit. For this reason, we cannot gain an understanding of Pentecostal teachings unless we grasp the significance of the Pentecostal point of view or "hermeneutic." Please note:

> "Pentecostals have understood that the Scriptures can be interpreted properly only through the agency of the Holy Spirit (cf. John 14:26; 16:13). Convinced of the importance of the Holy Spirit to the interpretative process, they bear a distinctive witness to an experience and life in the Spirit, out of which Pentecostal hermeneutics have emerged" (Burgess, McGee, and Alexander 1988, 376).

From this perspective, the Holy Spirit becomes the new *power source*, who enables believers to perform Christ's work in the earth and the *internal gyroscope*, who purifies their hearts and guides them into all truth. We shall examine the comprehensive work of the Holy Spirit in the next chapter.

Pentecostalism did not initially develop its own clearly defined theology. It continued, instead, as a twentieth-century adaptation of the Keswick (holiness) and Wesleyan revivals (Burgess, McGee, and Alexander 1988, 378). Pentecostal doctrine, therefore, follows the normative Christian pattern, with special emphasis being placed upon the *baptism in the Holy Spirit as the distinguishing feature of the movement.* A clearer "doctrinal distinctive" begins to emerge, however, when we examine what early Pentecostals believed and taught.

It has been previously mentioned that there has been, since the beginning, a "Pentecostal preference" for interpreting Scripture. As far as Pentecostals are concerned, Luke's historical accounts of the events and phenomena of the first-century Church are not history at all, but are demonstrations of the way things *ought to be* in the Church. Pentecostals ought to be holy, to lay hands on the sick and see them recover; they ought to prophesy and restore sight to the blind. Believers expect to perform exorcisms and tread on serpents. But before all these things, they expect to speak in tongues!

An excellent example of this "ought to be" ideology is found in a statement by Charles F. Parham, the "Father of Modern Pentecostalism." Writing in 1902, Parham declared:

> "Christ did not leave his believing children without signs of distinction to follow them that the world might know who were Christians and who were not. Neither did he send forth his servants to preach vague speculative theories of a world to come, but with mighty power for the relief of suffering humanity; feeding the hungry, clothing the naked; healing the sick; casting out devils; speaking with new tongues; confirming the word of inward benefit—wrought in Jesus Christ—by these outward visible signs" (see Dayton 1987, 24-25).

For Parham and others, the power of the living Christ had been poured out upon a brand new wave of Christians. These "special agents" of God's Kingdom had been chosen to demonstrate the mighty power of the Holy Spirit throughout the world. The essence of Parham's declaration—*God's power should be demonstrated in the Church*—is at the heart of Pentecostalism today.

Pentecostalism and the Full Gospel

Pentecostal preaching is designed to be simple and straightforward. The substance of the message is embodied in a four-pronged argument regarding the redemptive life, ministry, and work of Jesus Christ. In the Pentecostal framework, Jesus is seen as Savior and

Sanctifier, Healer, Baptizer in the Holy Spirit, and returning King. This doctrine has been a continuing staple of the Pentecostal diet.

Aimee Simple McPherson, early Pentecostal pioneer and founder of the International Church of the Foursquare Gospel, has been described as, "...the most prominent woman leader Pentecostalism has produced to date" (Burgess, McGee, and Alexander 1988, 571). Mrs. McPherson was among the first to articulate this fourfold Pentecostal "apologetic," when in 1922, she preached that:

> "Jesus saves us according to John 3:16. He baptizes us with the Holy Spirit according to Acts 2:4. He heals our bodies according to James 5:14-15. And Jesus is coming again to receive us unto Himself according to 1 Thessalonians 4:16-17" (Burgess, McGee, and Alexander 1988, 570; also see Dayton 1987, 21).

This Pentecostal hermeneutic forms the basis for all ministry. Unfortunately, what was, at first, a four-pronged foundational statement, has been interpreted in a variety of ways by those within the movement and applied to everyday practice.

The following questions are examples of the ongoing interpretational debates within the Pentecostal community: (1) Does Jesus save completely and instantly, or is sanctification a gradual process? (2) Can one who has been saved be lost again? (3) If speaking in other tongues is the only evidential sign of Spirit baptism, what of those who claim this grace, but who reject tongues? (4) Is healing limited only to the Divine intervention of God, or should medical science be considered as an element in the healing process? (5) When Jesus returns, will He come back in bodily form or has He already been revealed in a spiritual form, within the life of the Church? (6) Will the Rapture of the Church occur before or after the Tribulation?

Questions such as these are not mere speculations, worthy of a few moments of harmless conversation among friends. To the contrary, they affect the way in which Pentecostals define life itself. They represent the critical "stuff" that Pentecostals deal with all the time. It should come as no surprise, then, that Pentecostalism is manifested in 14,000 different denominational groupings across the globe, all with varying answers to the above questions.

A common Pentecostal theme is, "Wherefore come out from among them, and be ye separate, saith the Lord..." (2 Cor. 6:17). Those within the movement promote the ideal that a life of holiness and sanctification (being set apart) is not only important but essential to one's acceptability before God. For most Pentecostals, *the good life* is a life of total dedication to God through obedience to Christ.

With the theological and doctrinal foundation laid, we may now develop a summary of the primary goals of Pentecostal believers. These are:

1. To confess the Lordship of Jesus Christ and be saved;
2. To be baptized in the Holy Spirit;
3. To demonstrate the same giftings and power as Christ, in this modern era;
4. To demonstrate the lifestyle of Christ to the world;
5. To witness to and win lost souls for Christ;
6. To anticipate the physical appearing of Christ and the Rapture of the Church;
7. To share in the eternal rule of Christ throughout the ages to come.

Water Baptism and Pentecostal Practice

The ordinance of water baptism has been an integral part of Christian practice since the Church's beginning. Much more than a ritual, it is considered a vital element in the entire conversion process. Baptism is certainly not a "Christian only" concept. For example, under Judaism, baptism was practiced as a rite of initiation for Gentile proselytes or for other Jewish converts. But baptism holds a particular twofold significance for Christian believers: (1) Christ, by example, submitted to water baptism at the hands of John the Baptist (see Mt. 3:13-17; Mk. 1:9; Lk. 3:21); and (2) Christ commanded it for all believers (see Mt. 28:19; Mk. 16:15; Jn. 3:3-5; Acts 2:38-39).

All major Pentecostal denominations in the United States practice water baptism through immersion as part of the total conversion process (Burgess, McGee, and Alexander 1988, 654). Most, however, do not see baptism as a prerequisite to salvation. One is baptized, not *in order to be saved*, but as public confirmation of the fact that, as a result of personal repentance of a previous life of sin, and through a personal confession of the Lordship of Christ in one's life, he/she is *already saved*. The immersion of a believer in water does not wash away his/her sin. Neither does it cleanse, or otherwise deliver him/her from a sinful state. Horton and others emphasize that baptism is a means of identifying with the finished work of Christ and with His Body, the Church (Horton 1994, 558-559).

Water baptism by immersion accomplishes three major objectives. Through this ordinance, the believer: (1) identifies with the death, burial, and resurrection of Jesus Christ, recognizing that His sacrifice was made *in substitution* for that baptismal candidate; (2) publicly denounces his/her previous sin-dominated life and makes a commitment to live for Christ; and (3) demonstrates that he/she has been reborn into Christ and into the Church.

The majority of Pentecostals use a Trinitarian formula for baptism ("in the name of the Father, the Son, and the Holy Spirit"), yet Oneness believers baptize in the name of "Jesus only." In spite of these formulaic disagreements, both camps would agree with F.F. Bruce that, "The idea of an unbaptized Christian is simply not entertained in the New Testament" (See Horton 1994, 558).

A final item for consideration in this chapter is the doctrine of Oneness or "Jesus only" Pentecostalism. I focus on this issue, not to spread further dissension, but because Oneness Pentecostalism represents the theological door through which I entered the Kingdom of God.

Oneness Pentecostalism: A Theological Overview

In 1913, Frank J. Ewart first developed a theology of the name of Jesus and began to teach a "New Issue" doctrine regarding the oneness of the Godhead. Ewart and other prominent Pentecostal ministers such as Glenn A. Cook, Howard A. Goss, J. Roswell Flower, Garfield T. Haywood, and Andrew Urshan were among those who were re-baptized in water in Jesus' name (Burgess, McGee, and Alexander 1988, 644).

Between 1914 and 1918, a series of heated discussions regarding this issue occurred among Pentecostal leaders. As a result, the Pentecostal Assemblies of the World (P.A.W.), initially formed in 1906, was reorganized in 1918 as the first Oneness Pentecostal organization (Burgess, McGee, and Alexander 1988, 646). Since 1920, the Oneness wing has made up one-fourth (25 percent) of all Pentecostals in the United States. In addition, they are represented worldwide by some 90 denominations in 57 different countries (Burgess, McGee, and Alexander, 824).

Most Trinitarians and Unitarians (Jesus only) believe that the theological chasm that divides them is too wide and too deep to traverse. This issue is one of particular interest to me because the Oneness doctrine represents my earliest Pentecostal roots.

A Judeo-Christian Foundation

Oneness Pentecostalism (OP) is directed toward a Christocentric concept of God. In this view, Christ is totally God all by Himself, and He performs the functions of Father, Son, and Holy Spirit simultaneously and without interruption, throughout eternity. The Oneness model is a convergence of ideals in which two separate themes, one Jewish and one Christian, are utilized to develop a comprehensive, yet *economical* vision of God.

The first theme, originating under the Old Covenant, emphasizes the fact of the Oneness of God. In the Hebrew mind, God is One. It is in Judaism that we find the *Shema*, that states, "Hear O, Israel: The Lord our God is one Lord" (Deut. 6:4). This statement holds a place of preeminence in Jewish thought and culture. In fact, "Because of its emphasis on the unity of God, the Shema (Hebrew for 'hear') is considered the Jewish 'confession of faith' and a vital part of the liturgy…"(Werblowsky and Wigoder 1965, 365).

The second thematic element in the Oneness doctrine is established within the framework of the New Covenant. The belief is held that Jesus Christ is not just the Son of God, but He is the *Sum of God*. As such, He manifests God's total essence and character.

This position is based primarily on the Scripture in the Book of Colossians, where it is stated, "For in Him [that is, in Jesus] dwelleth all the fulness of the Godhead bodily" (Col. 2:9). In addition, John's Gospel records Jesus as having said, "I and My Father are one" (Jn. 10:30).

The Oneness ideology promotes the argument that Jesus Christ is not only the same as God, but that He is historically all that there ever was of God. Jesus singularly fulfills all the requirements to be God, by Himself. From this perspective, the names, "Father," "Son," and "Holy Spirit" are historical and analytical titles, used respectively to refer to particular roles that Jesus has played and will continue to play throughout eternity. Jesus is seen as the Father in creation, the Son in redemption, and the Holy Spirit in the outpouring of God's grace.

In the OP construct, the Holy Spirit is considered to be the *Spirit of God*, empowering us to live in accordance with God's will. But the Spirit is without a distinctive form, character, or personality. In my dad's church, we sang a song entitled, "Have You Got It [the Holy Spirit] Like the Bible Says?" In the OP tradition, all reference made to the Holy Spirit as "He," is always considered to be metaphorical rather than actual in nature. In the Oneness format there is room in the character of God for Jesus only.

The Christocentric vision of OP provides an exciting, although particularistic, framework for validating the Lordship of Christ. Oneness proponents hold that Christ can never be identified simply as a participating member of the Godhead. Instead, the fullness of God's identity must conclude *with Christ alone.*

This brief summary was not meant to be an exhaustive examination of Oneness Pentecostalism. Neither was it my purpose to condemn any group or denomination that exalts Christ. Rather, I have attempted to present my understanding of the theological door through which I entered the Kingdom of God. The teaching that I received in the OP denomination helped to formulate my earliest values as a child and provided a foundation upon which I continue to develop a dynamic relationship with God.

Conclusion

This chapter has provided a descriptive overview of the basic tenets of Modern Pentecostalism. It is designed to alert us to the fact that Pentecostalism is a dynamic move of God through which He expresses His redemptive purpose. But even in our role as students, we cannot help but feel the excitement that comes from knowing we are included in God's plans for the future.

I remain Pentecostal in spirit, intent, and practice. But I hasten to say that the Pentecostal faith will only continue to fulfill its God-given mandate to the degree that it: (1) increases our knowledge of God, (2) enhances our fellowship with God, and (3) inspires us to become the eternal brightness of God's glory in Jesus Christ.

Beginning with Chapter 5, we shall turn our attention to the historical evolution of the Pentecostal phenomenon. Our immediate reference will not be the Modern Pentecostal Revival or the Day of Pentecost itself. Our investigation will, instead, take us back to a time and place when *Pentecost* first erupted among a nation of Jewish slaves. This excursion into the past is taken, not just to inform us, but so that God's Kingdom will be advanced among us.

Challenge Questions:

1. In what ways might Pentecostals benefit from a better understanding of the nature of the Pentecostal phenomenon?
2. How may Pentecostals be convinced that it is God's will for us to function as a part of the Church?
3. In what ways should Pentecostal theology differ from/be the same as normative Christian doctrine?
4. What are some of the significant benefits to Holy Spirit baptism, beyond those of conversion and sanctification?
5. How can we, in Pentecost, clarify the Pentecostal mandate so that we and the rest of the world will understand and embrace it?

References:

Barrett, David B. "A Survey of the 20th-Century Pentecostal/Charismatic Renewal in the HolySpirit, With It's Goal of World Evangelization." Burgess, Stanley M., Gary B. McGee, and Patrick H. Alexander, eds. *Dictionary of Pentecostal and Charismatic Movements*. Grand Rapids, MI: Zondervan Publishing House, 1988.

Dayton, Donald. *Theological Roots of Pentecostalism*. Metuchen, NJ, and London: Scarecrow Press, Inc., 1987.

Horton, Stanley M., ed. *Systematic Theology*. Springfield, MO; Logion Press, 1994.

Johns, Cheryl Bridges. "The Adolescence of Pentecostalism: In Search of a Legitimate Sectarian Identity," *PNEUMA: The Journal of the Society for Pentecostal Studies*, 17:1: 3-17, 1995.

McDonnell, Kilian. "Improbable Conversations: The International Classical Pentecostal/Roman Catholic Dialogue," *PNEUMA: The Journal of the Society for Pentecostal Studies*, 17:2 Fall 1995: 163-188.

Menzies, Willilam. *Anointed to Serve*. Springfield, MO: Gospel Publishing House, 1971.

Zwi Werblosky, R.J., and Geoffrey Wigoder, eds. *The Encyclopedia of the Jewish Religion*. New York, Chicago, San Francisco: Holt, Rinehart, and Winston, Inc., 1965.

Chapter 5

Going Back to the Old Landmark

Three times in a year shall all thy males appear before the Lord thy God in the place which he shall choose; in the feast of unleavened bread, and in the feast of weeks, and in the feast of tabernacles: and they shall not appear before the Lord empty (Deuteronomy 16:16).

Modern Pentecostalism finds its biblical origins in the nation of Israel before the cross and in the New Testament Church after the cross. Therefore, as we attempt to clarify the mandate for the current Pentecostal Movement, we need to look back at our beginnings to find the seeds of our existence that were planted by Almighty God.

In this chapter, we shall examine the advent of Pentecost within the context of three feasts prominent in Jewish history, locating the fulfillment of the feasts in the New Testament, and extracting some relevant truths that apply to the Modern Pentecostal Movement. Although the word, *Pentecost* (Greek for "fiftieth") does not appear at all in the Old Testament and only three times in the New Testament, the Pentecostal ethos is well-rooted in the historical experience of God's people. It carries great significance, therefore, both for Israel, who the apostle Paul called, "...the church in the wilderness" (Acts 7:38a), and for the Church of the New Testament. In tracing the biblical themes that form the basis for the Pentecostal phenomenon, we shall rely heavily upon the work done by Kevin J. Connor in his book, *The Feasts of Israel*.

The Feasts of the Lord

In the earliest days of Israel's history, God established three commemorative feasts for the Hebrew nation to observe. These were the Feast of Unleavened Bread (Passover), the Feast of Weeks (Pentecost), and the Feast of Tabernacles. The three feasts were actually seven separate feasts, and though they had distinctive features, they held these seven attributes in common:

- All were feasts of the Lord. He instituted them and gave instructions for how and when they would be observed;
- All were established to commemorate a specific aspect of Israel's development as the chosen people of God;
- All were harvest feasts designed to coincide with the annual planting and reaping cycle of the Hebrew agricultural society;
- Only the males were to attend as they were the heads of the Jewish households;
- All who participated in the feasts had to bring an offering according to their ability to give;
- All three feasts were observed literally by the nation of Israel in the Old Testament; and
- All were designed to be realized spiritually by Christ, by the New Testament Church corporately, and by each believer.

A summary outline of the feasts is provided in chapter 23 of Leviticus and in other pertinent Old Testament passages. A brief description follows.

1. **The Feast of Unleavened Bread: "A New Beginning."** (Note: Selected Old Testament references: Exodus 12:1-12,21-29; Leviticus 32:4-5; Numbers 33:3; Deuteronomy 16:1-8. New Testament references include: Matthew 26:1-2,17-75; 27:1-66; Mark 14:15; Luke 22-23: John 18–19; Hebrews 11:28.)

a. **Old Testament:** The Israelites had been in bondage to the Egyptians for a period of 400 years when God commissioned Moses to lead them into the land of Canaan. God prepared His chosen people for a new relationship with Him. First, He established a new "sacred calender year" for the Israelites to observe. The Jewish New

Year began in the seventh month of the civil calender year at that time. God then gave Moses specific instructions on how the Israelites were to prepare for their departure from Egypt.

On the fourteenth day of the first month, the Israelites were to kill an unblemished lamb and spread its blood over the lintels and doorposts of their houses as a means of identification. The meat of the lamb was to be roasted and prepared with bitter herbs and unleavened bread. The members of each household were to eat the *Passover* meal hastily in anticipation of their imminent departure from Egypt.

God warned that on that same night He would send a death angel and kill all the firstborn, both human and animal, throughout the land of Egypt. But He promised the Israelites that, "...the blood shall be to you for a token upon the houses where ye are: and when I see the blood, I will pass over you, and the plague shall not be upon you to destroy you..." (Ex. 12:13). Then God instructed Moses that, "...this day shall be unto you for a memorial; and ye shall keep it a feast to the Lord throughout your generations; ye shall keep it a feast by an ordinance for ever" (Ex. 12:14).

Passover was to be celebrated during the first month of the sacred year. The Feast of Passover consisted of three separate feasts: The actual *Feast of Passover* commemorated the salvation of Israel by means of a blood sacrifice (see Lev. 23:4-5); The *Feast of Unleavened Bread* required the cleansing of each household of all leaven as a means of consecration and separation of the nation unto the Lord (see Lev. 23:6-8); and the *Feast Day of the Sheaf of Firstfruits* involved a dedication to the Lord of the firstfruits of the harvest (see Lev. 23:9-14). In summary, the entire Passover Feast celebrated the salvation of Israel from Egyptian bondage and the beginning of their new life in relationship with God.

b. **New Testament:** In the New Testament, Christ fulfilled the requirements of Passover through His substitutionary death, burial, and resurrection. First, *Christ is the Passover Lamb* who shed His innocent blood at Calvary in payment for our sins. He is the Lamb of God who was slain before the foundation of the world (see Jn. 1:29;

Rev. 5:6-9; 13:8). Second, *Christ is the Unleavened Bread* whose sinless life was given to nurture us and whose flesh was broken to cleanse us unto righteousness (see Mt. 26:26-27; Mk. 14:22-26; Lk .22:15-20; Jn. 6:33-35;51-56; 1 Cor. 11:23-25). Third, *Christ is the Sheaf of the Firstfruits* who, through His resurrection, became the *firstfruits* of all who have died and will die in Him, and who ascended to Heaven, presenting Himself as the *First Sheaf of dedication*, to be waved before the Father at His throne (see 1 Cor. 15:20-23). This is why Christ could say with boldness, "...I am the resurrection and the life: he that believeth in me, though he were dead, yet shall he live" (Jn. 11:25).

Today, Passover serves as a reminder, both to Israel and to the Church, of the accomplishment of God's redemptive plan by means of the ultimate *blood sacrifice*. A new beginning takes place for all who will accept Christ's sacrifice as payment for their sins. Believers are reminded of the sacredness of Passover each time they partake of the Lord's Supper, which Jesus instituted before His crucifixion (see Mt. 26:26-28; Mk. 14:22-25; Lk. 22:15-20: 1 Cor. 11:23-25).

2. **The Feast of Weeks: "The Birth of a Nation."** (Note: Old Testament references: Exodus 19-20,24; Deuteronomy 16:9-12; Exodus 23:16-17; 34:22-23; Leviticus 23:15-21; Numbers 28:26-31. New Testament findings: Acts 2; 2 Corinthians 3; Hebrews 8.)

a. **Old Testament:** The Israelites escaped from Egypt, crossed the Red Sea, and proceeded to Mt. Sinai. God called Moses up the mountain and instructed him to sanctify the people, thus preparing them to receive the Word of God. On the fiftieth day after Passover, God gave Moses the Ten Commandments and most of the balance of the Law. Speaking through Moses, God said,

Ye have seen what I did unto the Egyptians, and how I bare you on eagles' wings, and brought you unto Myself. Now therefore, if ye will obey My voice indeed, and keep My covenant, then ye shall be a peculiar treasure unto Me above all people: for all the earth is Mine: and ye shall be unto Me a kingdom of priests, and an holy nation... (Exodus 19:4-6).

In response to God's offer, the Israelites said to Moses, "...All that the Lord hath spoken we will do..." (Ex. 19:8). As they entered the covenant, they accepted all the conditions that God established for them to maintain fellowship with Him. The *Feast of Weeks* was instituted to commemorate: (1) the giving of the Mosaic Law; and (2) the birthday of Judaism. It also celebrated Israel's freedom from Egyptian bondage and a new life in covenant with God.

The Feast of Weeks, which was to be celebrated in the third month of the sacred year, was so named because it was to occur seven weeks (7 x 7 days plus one day), or fifty days following the waving of the sheaf of firstfruits in the Passover celebration. It was also known as he *Feast of Harvest* (see Ex. 23:16); the *Day of Firstfruits* (see Num. 28:26; Ex. 34:22); the *Feast of Harvest, the Firstfruits of Wheat Harvest* (Ex. 34:22); and the *Feast of Harvest, the Firstfruits of Israel's labours* (Ex. 23:16) (See Connor 1980, 34). In the land of Canaan, it was to occur at the time of the first harvest of the year, that being the wheat harvest. This would come as a result of the Spring or early rain and the second, the fruit harvest, would follow the latter rain at the end of the harvest season.

Every seventh year in Israel was to be a Sabbatical year, a period in which the land was to be rested from all planting, and God Himself would provide for the needs of the people (see Lev. 25:1-7). Every fiftieth year (7 x 7 Sabbatical years, plus one year) was to be known as the year of *Jubilee*. During that year, not only was the land to be rested, but slaves were to be freed, debts cancelled, and liberty was to be proclaimed throughout the nation (see Lev. 25:8-17).

b. **New Testament:** The Feast of Weeks of the Old Testament became known as the *Feast of Pentecost* in the New Testament (see Acts 2; 20:16; 1 Cor. 16:8). At this point, we should take note of a characteristic of this feast that sets it apart from the Feast of Passover and from the third feast, that of Tabernacles.

Both Passover and Tabernacles were to be celebrated with unleavened bread only. God informed His people that anyone who did not observe this mandate was to be, "...cut off from the congregation of Israel, whether he be a stranger, or born in the land"

(Ex. 12:19). In Scripture, leaven generally stands for evil or for corrupting influences. Unleavened bread, then, was used to retain the integrity and purity of the sacrifices made unto the Lord. The Feast of Weeks (Pentecost), on the other hand, might have also been called a "Feast of Leaven," in that it was to be celebrated using two waves of *leavened bread.* In explaining the contrast, Connor says, "...Passover wholly speaks of Christ and His sinless perfection, while Pentecost has to do with the church, which has not as yet attained to sinless perfection" (Connor 1980, 38).

Based upon this assessment, we may conclude that the leaven in the wave loaf offering was indicative of the leaven or "imperfection" in Israel at that time and in the Church of today. While we possess the perfect life of Christ within us, we must still submit to the purging fire of the Holy Spirit, so that our motives, thoughts, and actions may be purified and transformed into the likeness of Christ.

Jesus, the Passover Lamb of God, after overcoming Calvary and the grave, embarked on a post-resurrection ministry that lasted 40 days. On the day of His ascension to the Father, Jesus told His disciples that they would not be left comfortless, and He promised to send the Holy Spirit to work among them in their future endeavors. Jesus instructed His followers to return to Jerusalem and wait for the outpouring of the Holy Spirit.

Ten days later (50 days following the resurrection), the Feast of Pentecost was being celebrated in Jerusalem. On that day, 120 Jewish believers were gathered in the upstairs of a house praying and seeking God. At Mt. Sinai, their Old Testament predecessors had escaped from the bondage of Egyptian servitude. And now, in Jerusalem ("Mt. Zion"), these individuals confessed Christ and were baptized in His name. They were also baptized in the Holy Spirit and were liberated, not from bondage to Egypt, but from enslavement to satan's law of sin and death.

Just as the giving of the Mosaic Law marked the birthday of Judaism, so the Day of Pentecost signified: (1) *the writing of the law of God on the hearts and minds of the believers* (see Jer. 31:31-34; Heb. 8);

and (2) *the birthday of the Church* (see Acts 2). Luke recorded the consummation of the *New Covenant* as it occurred in the upper room:

And suddenly there came a sound from heaven as of a rushing mighty wind, and it filled all the house where they were sitting. And there appeared unto them cloven tongues like as of fire, and it sat upon each of them. And they were all filled with the Holy Ghost, and began to speak with other tongues, as the Spirit gave them utterance (Acts 2:2-4).

Word of this incredible event spread quickly throughout the streets of Jerusalem. As Jews from various nations gathered and heard the praises of God being spoken in their own languages, their reactions were mixed. Many were astounded, perhaps thinking that this was God's way of reversing the events at Babel, when He created several languages out of one (see Gen. 11:9). In contrast, some of the more cynical onlookers said, "These men are full of new wine" (Acts 2:13b). Peter the apostle, seeing the wonderment among the crowd, assured them that they were not watching a drunken party. He stood up and said, "...these [men] are not drunken, as ye suppose.... But this is that which was spoken by the prophet Joel" (Acts 2:15-16).

Peter then described this current ecstatic event as a fulfillment of God's promise given to Joel hundreds of years earlier:

...And your sons and your daughters shall prophesy, and your young men shall see visions, and your old men shall dream dreams: and on My servants and on My handmaidens I will pour out in those days of My Spirit; and they shall prophesy (Acts 2:17-18; see also Joel 2:28-29).

Following Peter's delivery of the first Pentecostal sermon, the experience of the original 120 was shared that same day by an additional 3,000 people (see Acts 2:41). A few days later, 5,000 more received the baptism in the Holy Spirit (see Acts 3:4). From that time forward, Pentecost has been available to the Church and to individual believers.

The resurrection of Christ (Passover) and the outpouring of the Holy Spirit (Pentecost) represent the two foundational events of the Christian Church. As Pentecost under the Old Covenant occurred subsequent to Passover, so must Holy Spirit baptism naturally follow the new birth in the New Testament. As Connor says:

"Passover is but the beginning, introducing one to the Lamb of God, Jesus Christ. The believer must continue on in the Feasts of the Lord and enter into Pentecost. Pentecost brings one into the blessed ministry of the Holy Spirit and into the church, the Body of Christ. However, this Feast is not the ultimate. There is another Feast into which the believer and the church must enter. This is the Feast of Tabernacles" (Connor 1980, 42).

3. **Tabernacles: "The Greatest of All Feasts."** (Note: Old Testament scriptural references: Leviticus 23:23-44; Numbers 29:1-40; 10:1-10; Leviticus 16. New Testament: the Book of Hebrews.)

a. **Old Testament:** The period after Passover and Pentecost, during the fourth, fifth, and sixth months, was a season in which very little rain fell. At the end of this period, in the seventh sacred month, came the latter rains and the final harvest of the year, the fruit harvest. The Feast of Tabernacles was to be celebrated at the end of this final harvest (see Lev. 23:33-34). According to Connor, "The Feast of Tabernacles, or Booths pointed back to Israel's first encampment after their Exodus from Egypt, as they encamped on the edge of the Wilderness (Exod. 12:37; Num. 33:1-6)" (Connor 1980, 66).

Like Passover, Tabernacles consisted of three separate feasts. These included the following: (1) The *Feast Day of Trumpets*, a festival of trumpets in which the nation was called to prepare for the coming Day of Atonement (see Lev. 23:23-25); (2) The *Feast Day of Atonement*, the most solemn of all feasts in which God would cleanse the nation and the sanctuary (see Lev. 23:26-32); and (3) The *Feast Day of Tabernacles*, the most joyous feast of all during which the people of Israel would leave their homes and rejoice before the Lord because He had delivered them from Egypt.

All three feasts—Passover, Weeks, and Tabernacles—were to be celebrated annually, once the children of Israel had reached Canaan. Unfortunately, a spirit of unbelief developed within them that stopped their pursuit into Canaan. At Kadesh-Barnea, the Israelites became fearful that they would not be able to invade the land of Canaan, even though God had already promised them victory (see Num. 13:26-33). As a result, they rebelled against God and His servant, Moses (see Num. 14:1-14).

The Israelites had experienced the lifesaving victory of Passover. They had celebrated Pentecost, receiving the Law and witnessing the birth of the Jewish religion. But that first wave of God's people would forfeit their right to celebrate the greatest feast of all, that being Tabernacles. At the order of God, they endured 40 years of wilderness wanderings, and He raised up an entirely new generation to go into Canaan (see Num. 14:22-37). Of the original Israelite population that left Egypt, only Joshua and Caleb shared in the blessing of those who were obedient to the will of God (see Num. 14:30). It would be left to future generations to celebrate all three of the sacred feasts of the Lord.

b. **New Testament:** Under the New Covenant, The Feast of Tabernacles has been fulfilled in Christ but not in His Body, the Church (see the Book of Hebrews). In the four Gospels, Christ is seen as the fulfillment of the Feast of Passover, Unleavened Bread, and the Sheaf of Firstfruits. The Book of Acts reveals the fulfillment of Pentecost, first in Christ and then in the Church. There is a growing sentiment that the Church as a modern version of Old Testament Israel can expect to celebrate the Feast of Tabernacles on the other side of our own "wilderness wanderings."

As we near the end of the Church Age, we are on the threshold of experiencing the greatest feast of all. Connor points out that the Feast of Tabernacles, "...sets forth the gathering of the saints unto the Lord, the perfection of the church by the power of blood atonement, and the final harvest of souls before Christ comes" (Connor 1980, 72). As a summary note, I would offer that this current period, which we typically refer to as the Church Age, is in reality, the *Age of the Holy Spirit.*

The Church Age: The Age of the Holy Spirit

When Jesus was nearing the end of His own ministry, He promised His followers that the Holy Spirit would come and empower them to replicate the work that Jesus had done. Jesus called Him: the Comforter (see Jn. 16:7), another Comforter (see Jn. 14:16), the Spirit of truth (see Jn. 14:17), and the Holy Ghost (see Jn. 14:26).

On the Day of Pentecost, when the Holy Spirit descended as cloven tongues upon 120 souls waiting in the upper room (see Acts 2:1-4), He unleashed the limitless power of God upon the earth. Since that time, the extensive phenomena related to Holy Spirit baptism have been exciting to some and threatening to others. And though His mission has not yet been fully accomplished, the Holy Spirit has come to infuse the Church with a fresh anointing of God's grace.

The Executor of God's Estate

Later in this text, we shall address the subject of the Bible as a written contract between God and His people. The Bible records the provisions of God's promise to share the wealth of His inheritance with those who enter into New Covenant fellowship with Him. The Holy Spirit has been chosen to serve as Executor of the New Covenant, coordinating the operation of the New Testament Church. The Spirit does not challenge the authority of Jesus but glorifies and testifies of Him (see Jn. 15:26; 16:14). For the Spirit knows, as do we, that the Church is Christ's.

Jesus gave a glimpse of the Holy Spirit's scope of authority saying, "And when He comes He will reprove [convict] the world of sin, and of righteousness, and of judgment" (Jn. 16:8). Particularly, the Spirit has been charged to execute a number of responsibilities (see Fig. 5.1). These are:

- Draw persons to and establish them in Christ (see Jn. 6:44; 1 Cor. 12:13);

- Baptize believers into Christ and into the Church (see Jn. 3:5; 1 Cor. 12:13);
- Endow believers with power to perform the works of Christ and to live like Christ (see Lk. 24:49; Acts 1:8; Jn. 14:12);
- Bring comfort (see Jn. 14:16; Acts 9:31);

(Fig. 5.1) **RESPONSIBILITIES OF THE HOLY SPIRIT**

- Guide believers into all truth (see Mt. 16:17; Jn. 14:26; 16: 13-14; Rom. 8:14);
- Convict the world of sin, righteousness, and judgment (Jn. 16:8);
- Dispense spiritual gifts in the Church (see 1 Cor. 12:1-11);
- Provide intercessory prayer for the Church (see Rom. 8:26); and
- Manifest Christ's fruit in the Church (see Phil. 1:11; Gal. 5:22-23).

Implications for the Pentecostal Movement

In fulfilling these responsibilities, the Holy Spirit has begun to intensify His efforts to prepare the Church to meet the Lord. Right now, He holds in His hand a "spiritual chisel," with which He is pruning and perfecting those within the Body of Christ. He has already begun to chip away at the crusty barnacles of ignorance, fear, and unbelief that encase our human hearts. He is working feverishly within us, striking against everything that now hinders our growth in Christ. He is working to fulfill His task of perfecting us and molding us into Christ's image.

I believe that the Spirit is knocking huge, gaping holes into our incomplete and incorrect theologies. He is stamping out the fear that has gripped us and that has caused us to run from the holiness of God. He, the *Spirit of truth*, is redefining our perception of truth, and He is filling us with a renewed understanding of who we really are in God and in Christ. The Spirit is revealing the person and purpose of the living Christ to all who desire to see. Furthermore, He is shaking the walls of bigotry and division that have plagued the Church since *the day after* the Day of Pentecost. The Holy Spirit is awakening us to the fact that He is that power that lives in us and that enables us to become all that God has ordained us to be...not just someday, in the sweet by and by...but today.

Where Do We Go From Here?

Much of what God has promised to believers today is going unclaimed because we have not yet seen ourselves in the image of Jesus Christ, who is our Savior, our Healer, our Baptizer in the Holy Spirit, and our soon coming King! We have before us the opportunity to progress to new levels of development in God and to experience a greater degree of fulfillment of His promises within us. Connor offers a challenging comparison between our experience and that of Israel before us:

"The nation of Israel wandered for 40 years; the Church has been wandering for approximately 40 Jubilees (40 x 50 = 2,000 years). But the wilderness wanderings are coming to an end. A new generation is arising. They are experiencing Christ as their

Passover. They are keeping the Feast of Pentecost in the Baptism of the Holy Spirit and the formation of the Church. They will not stop there but will move on and experience the Feast of Tabernacles and the truths symbolized therein." (Connor 1980, 45)

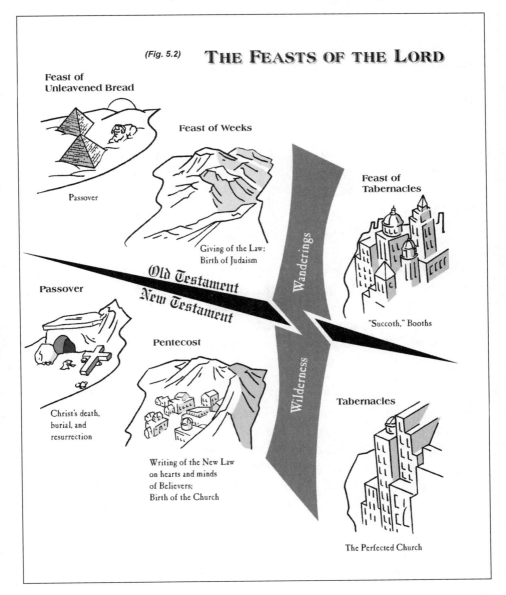

(Fig. 5.2) THE FEASTS OF THE LORD

Feast of Unleavened Bread

Feast of Weeks

Feast of Tabernacles

Passover

Giving of the Law; Birth of Judaism

Old Testament

New Testament

Wanderings

Passover

"Succoth," Booths

Pentecost

Wilderness

Tabernacles

Christ's death, burial, and resurrection

Writing of the New Law on hearts and minds of Believers; Birth of the Church

The Perfected Church

Conner points to the fact that it is God's will for believers in this generation to experience all three feasts of the Lord right now. Whether or not we do this is a matter of our choice. It is left up to us to examine our current Christian experience to determine whether we are still progressing or whether we have stopped (see Fig. 5.2).

We may be satisfied with a Passover experience, having received salvation by the grace of God. In this case, we will not progress into Pentecost where we may reap the blessed effects of Holy Spirit baptism. Moreover, we may have been baptized in the Holy Spirit, and becoming so excited with our empowerment and our new spiritual gifts, we may have failed to pursue the perfection that God can work in us through the Feast of Tabernacles. God has offered it all to us: salvation, deliverance, healing, and eternal life. I say, "Let's take it all, just as He has offered it."

Conclusion

In this chapter, we have established the biblical foundation for the Feast of Pentecost and for the Modern Pentecostal Movement. Although we have reviewed the Feast of Unleavened Bread (Passover), the Feast of Weeks (Pentecost), and the Feast of Tabernacles, our attention for this text was focused upon Pentecost. As it has been shown, all three feasts of the Lord hold tremendous significance, both for Israel and for the Church, in relation to maintaining our fellowship with God.

At Mt. Sinai, God gave the Israelites the Mosaic Law, and Judaism was born. On the Day of Pentecost, God wrote His law on the hearts and minds of the 120 believers gathered in the upper room, and the Church was born. Holy Spirit baptism is designed to empower the Church and individual believers to replicate the life and ministry of Christ throughout the world.

At the beginning of the twentieth century, the early Pentecostal fathers experienced a modern-day outpouring of the Holy Spirit. In studying the Scriptures, they could see that the hand of God was turning the pages of history. They believed that they had lived to see and experience the "latter rain" of God's redemptive program and the final harvest of souls before the Rapture of the Church.

And now, as we near the end of this century, we need to pray that we will experience the solemn and joyous fulfillment of all three feasts of the Lord, and that we will be perfected in the image of our living Savior, Jesus Christ.

Challenge Questions

1. Why would the apostle Paul refer to Israel as "the church in the wilderness"?
2. From the information provided in this chapter, does it appear that non-believers are eligible to participate in celebrating the feasts of the Lord?
3. In celebrating the feasts of the Lord, much emphasis was placed upon recalling Israel's new beginnings with God. What might be the value to Pentecostals as we recall our own "new beginnings" with God?
4. Because Pentecost was just the second of Israel's three-phase harvest celebration, how does the end-time Church prepare for our experience of all three feasts of the Lord in our generation?
5. What principles might Pentecostals apply based upon an in-depth study of the feasts of the Lord?

References:

Connor, Kevin J. *The Feasts of Israel.* Portland, OR: Bible Temple Publishing, 1980.

Riggs, Ralph M. *The Spirit Himself.* Springfield, MO: Gospel Publishing House, 1949.

Part 3

Rebuilding the Broken Walls of Pentecostalism

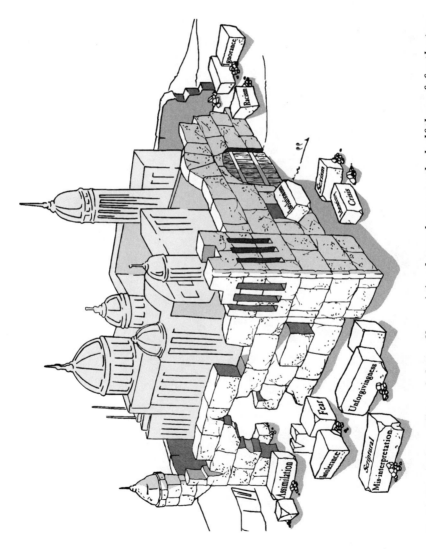

So built we the wall; and the wall was joined together unto the half thereof: for the people had a mind to work (Nehemiah 4:6).

Chapter 6

So What Happens After We Speak in Tongues?

For by one Spirit are we all baptized into one body, whether we be Jews or Gentiles, whether we be bond or free; and have been all made to drink into one Spirit (1 Corinthians 12:13).

The Continuing Wind of the Holy Spirit

We as Pentecostals have tended to view the birth of our movement as a cataclysmic event in which the Holy Spirit instantaneously fell upon us with the dawning of the twentieth century. It was noted in Chapter 4 that Pentecostalism, a unique expression of the Christian doctrine, actually developed out of a rich biblical heritage, established first in Israel and fulfilled on the Day of Pentecost. And even though it is the youngest of the modern Christian traditions, the Pentecostal model is established upon the prototype of the "Acts Church."

Since the Day of Pentecost, the powerful wind of the Holy Spirit has continued to blow upon the earth. Fr. Peter Hocken, a Spirit-filled Roman Catholic priest, has traced with precision the ongoing handiwork of the Holy Spirit. Hocken has cited the Spirit's influence in the following Christian movements:

- The monastic movement of the third and fourth centuries;
- The Celtic missionary movements of the sixth to eighth centuries;
- The monastic reform of the eleventh and twelfth centuries;

- The mendicant movements of evangelical simplicity in the twelfth and thirteenth centuries;
- The Hesychast movement in Greek Orthodoxy;
- The Carmelite reform associated with St. Teresa of Avila and St. John of the Cross;
- The French spiritual school of the seventeenth century;
- The Pietist and Moravian movements in seventeenth and eighteenth-century German Protestantism;
- The Wesleyan movement in eighteenth century Britain and the Great Awakening in North America;
- The nineteenth-century Haugean revival in Norwegian Lutheranism;
- The Welsh Revivals of 1859 and 1904; and
- The East African Revival from the 1930's... (Hocken 1994, 100-101).

This lengthy listing is a testimony to the fact that, as the Spirit has brooded over us throughout history, there have been those who were sensitive to the voice of the angel who said in the Book of Revelation, "He that hath an ear, let him hear what the Spirit saith unto the churches..." (Rev. 2:7). Convinced that their heritage was founded upon an unceasing tradition of faith, the early leaders of the Pentecostal Movement were not entirely surprised at the eruption of the Pentecostal fires in their day.

The Social Context of Modern Pentecostalism

As the nineteenth century came to a close, many social, cultural, and political forces were at work helping to create the climate for the eruption of the Modern Pentecostal Movement. The world at that time was both moving and changing at a fast rate. Note the observation made by D. William Faupel, Professor of Bibliography and Research at Asbury Theological Seminary:

"All are agreed that the changes which followed the American Civil War such as rapid industrialization, growing urbanization, and the Eastern European immigration had a profound effect upon the religious life of North America. In addition, such intellectual developments as Charles Darwin's theory of natural selection, William James' theory of education, the challenge of philosophical idealism to the prevailing Scottish realism, and the rise of higher criticism in Germany wrought great change upon the religious scene as well" (Faupel 1993, 10).

Students of history always have an advantage when analyzing events of the past. It is easy for us to provide "rational" explanations for former times as we look back with 20/20 hindsight. Such is the case with the birth of Pentecostalism. It is not surprising that Dr. Faupel would say, "...although the initial Pentecostal leaders were unaware of these forces, they were the most significant factors in explaining how the Pentecostal Movement came into being" (Faupel 1993, 11). It is within the context of these seemingly unrelated events that the "Twentieth Century Reformation" began.

A New Day Of Pentecost

Official Pentecostal beginnings in the United States may be traced back to 1900 and to the efforts of Charles F. Parham, an independent holiness evangelist. Parham described the events that took place at his Bethel Bible College in Topeka, Kansas:

"In December of 1900 we had our examination upon the subject of repentance, conversion, consecration, sanctification, healing, and the soon coming of the Lord. We had reached in our studies a problem. What about the second chapter of Acts?...I set the students at work studying out diligently what was the Bible evidence of the baptism of the Holy Ghost" (see Dayton 1987, 20).

On January 1, 1901, a small group of Parham's students were waiting prayerfully for God to send the Holy Spirit, like He had in Acts chapter 2. Late in the evening, Ms. Agnes Ozman began to speak in the Chinese language and became the first person recorded to have received Spirit baptism in the United States (Burgess, McGee, and Alexander 1988, 660). Ms. Ozman gave this account of her experience:

"It was nearly 11 o'clock on the first of January when it came into my heart to ask that hands be laid upon me that I might receive the gift of the Holy Ghost. As hands were laid upon my head, the Holy Spirit fell on me and I began to speak in tongues, glorifying God...It was as though rivers of living water were proceeding from my innermost being" (see Davis 1983, 14).

Within a few days, others at the Bible school, including Parham himself, received the baptism in the Holy Spirit and spoke in tongues, thus experiencing the phenomenon that had initially taken place on the Day of Pentecost.

The tongues experience also marked the emergence of a developing Pentecostal theology, as Parham and his followers were convinced that this most recent Holy Spirit outpouring was a definite sign of the second coming of Christ. They looked forward with great anticipation to the Rapture or catching away of the Church (particularly the Church Pentecostal) out of the world and into the presence of Christ.

Tongues and Pentecostal Evangelism

In the typical Pentecostal experience, the new convert speaks *glossolalia* (the gift of tongues). Some of the early Pentecostals, however, thought that they had been miraculously endowed with the ability to speak in the language of other cultures. This phenomenon, known as *xenolalia*, involves speaking in a known language that is unknown to the speaker (Horton 1994, 654). The xenolalic experience appears to be the one shared by the believers in Acts chapter 2. As Jews from various nations observed and heard the 120 speak in tongues in the upper room, they asked, "And how hear we every man in our own tongue, wherein we were born?" (Acts 2:8)

Similarly, Charles Parham believed that this new gift was a tool for use in conducting worldwide evangelism, with all language barriers now removed. His viewpoint on this issue was made public in an interview that appeared in the *Kansas City Times* in February, 1901:

"The Holy Ghost knows all the languages of the world, and all we have to do is to yield ourselves wholly to God and the Holy Ghost and power will be given to us so that we can have such control of our vocal chords, that we can enter any country on earth and talk and understand language. The time is now at hand when we should all receive this gift of tongues" (See Goff 1992, 11).

Although the early Pentecostal converts met with little success in this regard, Charles Parham remained undaunted in his dream to evangelize the world.

God Sends a Messenger

Parham eventually moved his Bible school to Houston, Texas. In 1905, William Seymour, a black holiness preacher who had heard about speaking in tongues from a close friend, eagerly enrolled in Parham's Bible school.

Just a few years earlier (1896), the U.S. Supreme Court had ruled in *Plessy v. Ferguson* that it was legal to maintain separate but equal accommodations for blacks and whites. As a result of this and other segregationist policies, Seymour was prohibited from sitting in the classroom at the Bible school. Undeterred, he sat in the hallway and listened to Parham's teaching on the tongues experience. Later, after Seymour moved to Los Angeles, California, he also received the baptism in the Holy Spirit.

On April 14, 1906, Brother Seymour held his first evangelistic service in a renovated warehouse at 312 Azusa Street (Burgess, McGee, and Alexander 1988, 780). This was an era of Jim Crow laws, rampant segregation, and racism. And yet, in the midst of a climate that was unsympathetic to reconciliation, this one-eyed son of former slaves launched a soul-saving campaign of unprecedented proportions. For a period of several years, visitors came to the Apostolic Faith Mission from various parts of the United States and from foreign countries to receive the baptism in the Holy Spirit.

As a result of Seymour's pioneering efforts, other Pentecostal revivals sprang up in "...Jerusalem, India, China, Europe, South America, and the Islands at sea" (Burgess, McGee, and Alexander 1988, 781). The majority of the early Pentecostal movements throughout the world may be traced back to Seymour's Azusa Street ministry. But Pentecostalism was more than a social movement designed to bring about racial and cultural reconciliation. It was a new beam of light shining unto the world.

Pentecostalism and Christianity: Four Options

Beginning with the Azusa Street Revivals, God released a "fresh oil" upon the Church. But this new outpouring was a great surprise, and many in the Church were caught off guard not knowing quite how to respond. Since that time, a tension has existed between Pentecostals and other Christians regarding the turf that each should occupy in the ministry of the Church during the end-times. Early Pentecostal leaders believed that the latter rain of God had begun. They felt that God was preparing a remnant people who would spread the gospel in a new and dynamic way, and that within a short time, perhaps even weeks or months, Christ would return to recover His true, Spirit-filled Church.

I believe that there were four options available to our Pentecostal forefathers regarding how they might have defined themselves in relation to the Church:

1. *Reject the Christian Church and ignore her.* Pentecostals could have determined that the Pentecostal experience was God's way of discarding the Church and of raising up a new and separate breed of Spirit-filled believers;

2. *Correct the Church and transform her.* Pentecostals could have invaded the Church with the "real truth" of the gospel and attempted to change her into a relevant force for God;

3. *Respect the Church and restore to her.* Pentecostals could have honored the Church as the Body of Christ and sought to replenish the original authority and power that she had been given on the Day of Pentecost, thus adding a "fresh anointing" to an already rich tradition; or

4. *Reflect the Church and conform to her.* Pentecostals could have denied their own new experience, promoted the status quo of a dry orthodoxy, and followed in step with the rest of the Church.

I mentioned in the previous chapter my belief that God had preselected the third option as the one that we were to pursue. I must add, however, that this is not an original thought on my part, and that it did not take 96 years for this discovery to be made. The following statement written in 1913 reveals that some early leaders understood the vision of God clearly and that they defined the Pentecostal Movement from a restorationist perspective:

"During the Reformation God used Martin Luther and others to restore to the world the doctrine of justification by faith (Rom. 5:1). Later on the Lord used the Wesleys and others in the great holiness movement to restore the gospel of sanctification by faith (Acts 26:18). Later still he used various ones to restore the gospel of Divine healing by faith (Jas. 5:14-15), and the gospel of Jesus' second coming (Acts 1:11). Now the Lord is using many witnesses in the great Pentecostal movement to restore the gospel of the baptism with the Holy Ghost and fire (Luke 3:16; Acts 1:5) with signs following (Mark 16:17, 18; Acts 2:4; 10:44-46; 19:6; 1:1–28:31). Thank God we now have preachers of the whole gospel" (see Dayton 1987, 19-20).

One can only speculate whether or not this message was clearly understood by those within the Pentecostal family. Unfortunately, it was not understood in that way by mainline Christians who chose to define Pentecostalism as a "theological anomaly," a sort of weird happening. Their belief that Pentecostals were, for the most part, a group of fanatical non-Christians left very little room in which to negotiate a settlement for peaceful coexistence between these two religious elements.

The Movement's Continuing Development

We have seen that those who first experienced Holy Spirit baptism believed they were part of a select group who would spread the gospel throughout the world just prior to the second coming of Christ. The first ten years of the movement, therefore, were marked by a high-intensity push to get as many people as possible saved and ready for the Rapture. But before the movement could build up much momentum, sores of divisiveness began to open.

Pentecostalism's two main architects, Charles Parham and William Seymour, held totally different views regarding racial reconciliation.

The Apostolic Faith Mission began as an integrated work where people from all races and nationalities were actively involved. Blacks, Whites, Hispanics, Mexicans, Asians, men, and women all participated in this great missionary work.

Frank Bartleman, one of the early participants at the Mission, wrote, "The color line has been washed away by the Blood [of Christ]" (Burgess, McGee, and Alexander, 1988, 781). This certainly seemed to mark the early days of the movement. And although William Seymour would have agreed with Bartleman's assessment, Charles Parham would have said otherwise—and did. When Parham, "the Father of Modern Pentecostalism," and Seymour's mentor in the gospel, visited the Azusa Street Mission in late 1906, he was appalled at the interracial and intercultural mixture of the congregation. A few years later, reflecting upon his own views of race mixing, Parham would write:

> "Men and women, whites and blacks, knelt together or fell across one another, frequently, a white woman, perhaps of wealth and culture, could be seen thrown back into the arms of a big buck nigger, and held tightly thus as she shivered and shook in a freak imitation of Pentecost. Horrible, awful shame" (see Butler 1994, 8).

We can hardly be shocked at these comments, for they were typical of the racial climate of that day. It is unfortunate, but such sentiments are still expressed in some Pentecostal circles today.

By the time the Azusa Street fires had burned out, Pentecostal organizations were becoming separate and racially unequal. The North American arm of Pentecostalism was branded with a racist mark that we have never outgrown. Even though Parham and Seymour continued to work diligently in the movement, they operated in very different camps.

William Seymour is recognized unquestionably as the major force in the worldwide spread of the Pentecostal Movement. But in his day he was snubbed by many who felt that he did not fit their description of the man whom they wanted to follow. Cecil M. Robeck, Jr. is a Pentecostal scholar who has searched through the annals of Pentecostal history with a fine-toothed comb. He has con-cluded, "Clearly, Seymour may be credited with providing the vi-sion of the 'color-blind' congregation. His was a radical experiment that ultimately failed because of the inability of whites to allow for a sustained role for black leadership" (Burgess, McGee, and Alexan-der 1988, 36). Although the Azusa Street "experiment" may appear to some as a failure, I see it as a vision for human unity that was or-dained by God Himself. And it is a vision that will never die.

As the Pentecostal Movement continued to develop, more splintering occurred. Blacks and Whites maintained their separate organizations. In addition, further division developed over views concerning the identity of the Godhead. Trinitarian and Oneness Pentecostals separated early in the history of the movement, and these two groups have remained apart ever since. Other doctrinal disputes over such issues as divorce and remarriage, rules concern-ing the ordination of women, movie-going, dancing, and dress codes have served to factionalize the Pentecostal Movement in a se-vere manner. We shall look closer at this phenomenon in the next chapter.

Rejection of Pentecostals by mainstream Christians has been an enduring theme during the history of the movement. A common la-bel for early Pentecostals was that of "holy rollers," a term used to define those who allegedly rolled on the ground under the power of God. In spite of the fact that they leaned toward a Fundamental-ist theology, Pentecostals were ignored and resented, even by those in the Fundamentalist Movement. For example, Faupel reports that, "Pentecostalism was condemned by the World's Christian Fundamentals Association in 1928 as being 'unscriptural' and 'a menace in many churches and a real injury to sane testimony of Fundamental Christians' " (Faupel 1993, 24). As a result of this type of continual exclusion, Pentecostals were forced to establish exclu-sive organizations, and for some time, this seemed to be a workable strategy for the movement's survival.

As the Pentecostal Movement got a little older, the level of ex-citement among its followers seemed to diminish. As Faupel says,

"By the 1930s and 1940s...a sense of dryness settled over the Movement. First generation leaders were passing away. The second generation leadership, having risen through the ranks, left many feeling something to be desired. Many hungered for a recovery of the initial vision" (Faupel 1993, 24).

During the mid-1940's many Pentecostals, tiring of the outcast label they had been wearing within the general Christian community, decided to join forces with the larger and more powerful Evangelical Movement. Consequently, in 1948, the Pentecostal Fellowship of North America (PFNA) was formed as a subgroup of Evangelicalism. But even as Pentecostals pushed to find greater social acceptance, their own movement lacked internal unity. PFNA membership was open to Whites only, a condition that lasted for 46 years.

Throughout the 1950's and 1960's, Pentecostals struggled so much to gain societal acceptance that a distinctive Pentecostal identity almost totally disappeared. This trend to become part of the Evangelical mainstream has continued into the decade of the 1990's. It has certainly become a major source of concern among those in the movement who desire to return to a more separate Pentecostal character.

Where We Now Stand

Robeck has cited three characteristics of the Pentecostal Movement that have marked its brief but dynamic existence. First, although Pentecostals prefer to be known as a spiritual community of believers with no intention of joining a worldwide "religious system," we have become active in our own selective brand of affiliation. We are well represented in such organizations as the Pentecostal and Charismatic Fellowship of North America, the Pentecostal World Fellowship, the National Association of Evangelicals, the National Black Evangelical Association, and the World Evangelical Fellowship. This fact allows Robeck to conclude: "Pentecostals are ecumenical, but we don't know it" (Robeck 1993, 39).

Second, Robeck states, "Pentecostals are multi-cultural, but we haven't learned how to act like it without hurting one another"

(Robeck 1993, 45). He cites the pervasive problem of racism within the movement, noting, for example, that White Pentecostals tend to identify with the agenda of the Republican party (and the religious right), while Black Pentecostals are more likely to be in sympathy with the Democratic party. He adds that "...the Black Pentecostal Movement has in recent years become more self-consciously African, embracing some black theologies and liberation theologies, while White Pentecostals have been overfed on prosperity or health and wealth teachings" (Robeck 1993, 47).

Robeck's third observation is that, "Pentecostals are evangelistic, but we are frequently indiscriminate about the appropriate object(s) of our evangelistic efforts" (Robeck 1993, 51). Pentecostals tend to see all non-Pentecostals (including other Christians) as being spiritually destitute and, therefore, in need of enlightenment toward the "true gospel." This continues to be a source of tremendous offense among those who come into contact with us. Robeck challenges us, saying, "We Pentecostals need to reevaluate our indiscriminate evangelistic efforts so that they will build up the church rather than render it increasingly divided in the world" (Robeck 1993, 58).

Although Dr. Robeck's assessment may appear to some to be argumentative, it should serve as a useful tool for helping us as Pentecostals to find our way out of a serious identity crisis. The short but rich history of the Pentecostal Movement has been marked by all the normal growing pains of any such enterprise. As we struggle to find our rightful place in God's end-time Church, we must first concede that although we are undoubtedly an integral part of Christ's Body, we are not the entire Body.

We have much work to do within a short time period. I share in Dr. Faupel's assessment that, "...Pentecostalism has come to a crossroads and that within the next decade it will have to decide which course of direction it will choose" (Faupel 1993, 26).

Pentecostalism: A Single Part of the Whole Body

The Pentecostal Movement did not suddenly erupt, as we might otherwise suspect, from the void of some spiritual Dark Age.

God has been pouring out His Spirit all along and this modern version might more appropriately be called a "renewal of the Spirit," for that is truly what it is. Moreover, we must understand that our movement does not represent the totality of God's self-revelation and that we are not, nor have we ever been, the only true voice of God for the world.

God is One in nature, and the means of His expression are infinitely varied. So, while Modern Pentecostalism is not the only manifestation of Acts chapter 2, it is one of the many unique expressions of God's grace during the twentieth century. The Church is Christ's Body. We go where He goes. His accomplishments are ours. In Christ, there can be neither defeat nor death. There can only be complete victory.

In order for Pentecostals to secure our rightful place in God's plans for the future, we must function as part of Christ's entire Body. We must seek to "...come in the unity of the faith, and of the knowledge of the Son of God, unto a perfect man, unto the measure of the stature of the fulness of Christ" (Eph. 4:13). In short, we must strive to reflect the image of Christ. We have already been told that, "For as the body is one, and hath many members, and all the members of that one body, being many, are one body: so also is Christ" (1 Cor. 12:12). We must take seriously God's dream of a unified Body with a renewed intensity to "...press toward the mark for the prize of the high calling of God in Christ Jesus" (Phil. 3:14).

Conclusion

There is an exciting day ahead. The final soul-winning harvest of God is on the horizon. In this chapter, we have addressed briefly the dilemma facing the Modern Pentecostal Movement as it determines its particular role in the Church of the twenty-first century. Whether Pentecostals will seek to edify and enhance the Body of Christ is largely a matter of how we see ourselves fitting into the big theological picture. In the next chapter, we shall take a closer look at some of the main internal problems that we must address *before* our movement can attempt to be a blessing to the rest of the world.

Challenge Questions

1. In looking back, does it appear that early Pentecostal leaders interpreted correctly their place in the larger Body of Christ?
2. What steps might be taken by leaders within the Pentecostal Movement to help eradicate the current Pentecostal identity crisis?
3. What strategies might Pentecostals employ that would allow them to regain a high level of respectability within the Church at large?
4. Are there options that early Pentecostals might have pursued within the Church other than those mentioned in this chapter? If so, what are they?
5. In what ways might modern Pentecostals better understand their God-given mandate within the total spectrum of Christ's ministry?

References

Anderson, Robert M. *Vision of the Disinherited: The Making of American Pentecostalism.* New York, NY: Oxford University Press, 1979.

Burgess, Stanley M., Gary B. McGee, and Patrick H. Alexander, eds. *Dictionary of Pentecostal and Charismatic Movements.* Grand Rapids, MI: Zondervan Publishing House, 1988.

Davis, Clara. *Azusa Street Till Now: Eyewitness Accounts of the Move of God.* Tulsa, OK: Harrison House, 1983.

Dayton, Donald. *Theological Roots of Pentecostalism.* Metuchen, NJ and London: Scarecrow Press, Inc., 1987.

Faupel, D. William. "Whether Pentecostalism?" Twenty-second presidential address, Society for Pentecostal Studies, November 22, 1992. *PNEUMA: The Journal of the Society for Pentecostal Studies,* 15: Spring 1993:9-27.

Goff, James R., Jr. "Closing Out of the Church Age: Pentecostals Face the Twenty-First Century," *PNEUMA: The Journal of the Society for Pentecostal Studies*, 14:1, Spring 1992:7-21.

Hocken, Peter. *The Glory and the Shame*. Guilford Surrey: Eagle, an imprint of Inter Publishing Service, 1994.

Parham, Charles Fox. *Apostolic Faith*, Baxter Springs, KS (December, 1912), cited in Anthea Butler, "Walls of Division: Racism's Role in Pentecostal History," a paper presented at the Twenty-Fourth Annual Meeting of the Society for Pentecostal Studies, Wheaton, IL: November 10-12, 1994: 8.

Robeck, Cecil M., Jr. "Taking Stock of Pentecostalism: The Personal Reflections of a Retiring Editor," *PNEUMA: The Journal of the Society for Pentecostal Studies*, 15:1, Spring 1993:35-60.

Chapter 7

Pentecostalism: A House Divided

...Every kingdom divided against itself is brought to desolation; and every city or house divided against itself shall not stand (Matthew 12:25).

The Pentecostal Dilemma

Much confusion exists among Pentecostals regarding the specific role that we should be playing in the ministry of the endtimes. Recognizing the authority and power available to us through Holy Spirit baptism, we are faced with the dilemma of how we might re-establish our movement as a viable component of God's redemptive work in this dispensation.

In our beginnings, we developed a mind-set and pattern of living that created a counterculture apart from traditional Christianity. For example, most Pentecostals have long believed that unless one has experienced conversion, water baptism, sanctification, and the baptism in the Holy Spirit, he/she is not saved. As we have promoted this particularistic doctrine, we have driven away more people than we have drawn. In our attempts to preach what we thought to be the only correct revelation of God's will, we have developed a reputation for being judgmental and exclusionary. For this we paid the high price of being rejected by the religious establishment. As a result, it has been difficult for Pentecostals to gain wide acceptance as a group, although the Pentecostal experience itself has spread throughout the world.

I believe that God is calling us to refocus our spiritual eyesight. He is showing us the guideposts that lead toward the pathway of the resurrected life in Christ. We need to take up the mantle of our calling in God, which is to promote the fullness of Christ's life, made possible through the baptism in the Holy Spirit. It is time for us to take up our positions alongside others in God's spiritual strike force who are warring against lethargy and defeatism in this world.

In this chapter, we shall attempt to isolate four problem areas that Pentecostals must address if we are to continue to play a major part in the Spirit's continuing work. The selected problem areas are: (1) a general spirit of division among us, (2) the impact of racism, (3) the Unitarian/Trinitarian debate regarding the Godhead, and (4) a misrepresentation of the authority given to us by the Holy Spirit.

A Spirit of Division

It was mentioned in the previous chapter that many of our efforts to gain acceptance in the larger society have caused us to develop a watered-down version of our faith. We now suffer less from rejection and more from our own identity crisis. A real spirit of division seems to have gripped our hearts, and we are struggling to wrench ourselves free from its clutches.

Pentecostalism, in spite of its savory freshness, has experienced more splintering than any other modern Christian belief system. It has been noted that there are 11,000 Pentecostal and 3,000 Charismatic denominations throughout the world. Among the many causes of this radical division, none is greater than that of our insistence upon *particularistic* (personal and individual) interpretation of the Scriptures. Pentecostals and Charismatics hold widely diverse opinions concerning scriptural directives for the practice of our faith. The range of beliefs is as varied as the above-mentioned numbers would indicate. For example, I know of one group that prohibits women from going into a church with their heads uncovered, while another holds that it is a sin for a man to wear a wedding ring.

At one extreme are those who emphasize the literal interpretation of the Scriptures and a legalistic form of lifestyle and worship. Adherents to this line of thinking stress the need to live a holy (sin-free) lifestyle and to treat the natural world as though it were a contaminated environment that must be overcome. Persons may expect as much goodness from God as they earn and as much punishment from Him as they deserve, based upon their behavior. And at all costs, they must seek to miss the eternal and unquenchable flames of hell (*fire and brimstone mentality*).

At the other end of the theological spectrum are those who view the Bible as a totally spiritual document, only understood in the light of God-given revelation. The belief is also held that while we live in a natural body, we operate on a plane that transcends the earth realm. Thus, we can expect to live free from the effects of sickness, disease, poverty, depression, and other such natural phenomena. Those of this persuasion say that all believers have been equipped to achieve in this life everything that Jesus achieved in His ministry. They say that we are now the living, visible manifestation of Christ, who no longer exists in bodily form. Christ's former personal identity has been changed into the form of the visible Church. Heaven and hell are not actual places, and Jesus is no longer an actual person. There will be no second coming of Christ because He has already come in us.

Between these two polar positions, as one would expect, there are many variations in scriptural interpretation and application among Pentecostals. Issues of conflict are both great and small. Debate continues on such questions as: (1) What is the correct formula for conducting water baptism? (2) Do women have a right to become ordained ministers? (3) Is Holy Spirit baptism a prerequisite to salvation? (4) Is the sharing of the sacraments essential to maintaining our fellowship with God? (5) Are Pentecostals the only ones who are "really" saved? (6) Should Pentecostals actively promote an open and integrated society?

Many stress divine healing as the only acceptable means of cure and reject even a consideration that medical treatment is ordained and inspired by Almighty God. Luke, the writer of Luke and Acts, is recognized for his spiritual revelation but ignored for the fact that he was a physician. Often, when serious physical ailments appear,

God is expected to miraculously intervene, even when many conditions could have been easily resolved with medical or surgical treatment. My father, a Pentecostal pastor, refused to undergo heart bypass surgery and ended up dying of a heart attack. And it was not as though he were an unlearned man. He had a master's degree in psychology from a major university and was an astute Bible scholar, teacher, and spiritual leader.

Except You See Signs

On one occasion, a certain nobleman asked Jesus to come to his home and to heal his dying son. Jesus said to the man, "...Except ye see signs and wonders, ye will not believe" (Jn. 4:48). This man did not want an intimate relationship with Jesus. Instead, he wanted a miracle. He wanted a visible manifestation of Christ's power. The man insisted that if Jesus did not come to his house, his son would die. Instead of accompanying him, Jesus said, "Go thy way; thy son liveth" (Jn. 4:50a).

Something in the words that Jesus spoke ignited a sense of hope within that man's heart. As he started back home to see his son, his desperation turned into anticipation. On his way, he was met by his servants, who reported that his son had been healed. The servants indicated the time of his son's recovery and he realized that it had occurred at the very moment when Jesus had said, "...Thy son liveth" (Jn. 4:53a). He was then convinced that Jesus' words had made his son whole.

We, in the Pentecostal culture, have fallen prey to the "show me" mentality of the world. Our vision concerning God's purpose for us has been blurred. In losing our focus, we have been tempted to look for signs from God rather than to believe the Word of God. We are joining the millions who are saying, "Lord, we will believe You, if You show us a sign." In desperation, we are demanding that Jesus come to our "theological house" and perform a miracle, lest we die. The fragmentation that has resulted from this kind of misunderstanding has made the identification of a singular Pentecostal character almost impossible. And those who have suffered most from this tension between doctrine and real life are the unsuspecting souls who simply cannot make their theology work.

It is not uncommon to find among former Pentecostals those who believe that they have failed to overcome a particular habit or sin. Some who are still practicing the faith wonder why God has not sent a particular miracle that they need. And now, as though we were not already confused enough, we have been exposed to the *prosperity doctrine*. Those in this camp are promoting the philosophy that God, who owns the cattle on a thousand hills (see Ps. 50:10), desires to endow us with endless material and financial blessings. Again, many who have followed this teaching have been frustrated by their inability to obtain the items of their so-called inheritance. As a consequence, they are now left to question the legitimacy of their status with God.

As we search for the right formula, there are numerous so-called experts who are ready to give us the latest "word" from the Lord. Television and radio ministries air throughout the day and night offering a wide range of solutions to meet our every need. With each offer, of course, comes a request for us to plant a financial seed into that particular ministry. In addition, books (including this one), pamphlets, audio and video tapes abound, covering an endless list of subjects. Instruction is now available on how to get our prayers answered, how to guarantee our miracles, how to put our angels to work, and much more.

As an educator, I support the idea of seeking ways to negotiate this difficult journey called life. But no formula, procedure, doctrine, or creed can assure us of complete and uninterrupted happiness in this life. In addition, most of the situations that we face as obstacles and that we want God to remove are actually opportunities for us to allow His glory to be revealed from within. But that kind of victory only comes as a result of changing our minds. It is the fruit of our decision to be God's servants and to partner with Him.

The Impact of Racism

Among Pentecostals, no sin, past or present, should be considered a greater blight than that of the practice of racism. And yet racism is as much a part of the Pentecostal Movement, at least in North America, as is the baptism in the Holy Spirit.

In 1906, at William Seymour's Apostolic Faith Mission, integration was a common theme and practice. In an early issue of the Mission's magazine, *The Apostolic Faith*, it was stated that, "...God makes no difference in nationality. Ethiopians, Chinese, Indians, Mexicans and other nationalities worship together" (see Butler 1994, 7). This viewpoint was not shared by Seymour's spiritual mentor, Charles Parham, who stated in one of his early sermons:

> "The Old Testament distinction of the peoples of the earth remains almost the same today. The Hebrews, Jews, and the various descendants of the ten tribes—the Anglo-Saxons, High Germans, Danes, Swedes, Hindoo, Japanese, and Hindoo-Japanese of Hawaii, and these possess about all the spiritual power of the world. The Gentiles-French, Spanish, Italian, Greek, Russian, and Turkish. These are formalistic, and so are their descendants in all parts of the world. Heathen are mostly heathen still—the Negro, Malay, and Indian" (see Butler 1994, 3).

These two statements represent quite different viewpoints regarding whether Spirit baptism should result in cultural and racial reconciliation.

As separate denominations for Blacks and Whites sprang up, the racial tone of our development was set for generations to come. Cecil M. Robeck, church historian and practicing Pentecostal, has observed that beginning in the 1940's, White Pentecostals joined forces with the Pentecostal Fellowship of North America and the National Association of Evangelicals, while Blacks were left out. Fifty years later, no single White Pentecostal denomination has publicly denounced racism, either within its own ranks or within the larger society. Dr. Robeck offers that, "Most of the major Pentecostal denominations in the U.S. are highly segregated. Racism is a rampant problem in American Pentecostalism" (Robeck 1993, 46).

Today, the largest Classical Pentecostal organizations, both Trinitarian and Oneness, are almost all White and so far they appear to have done little that would drastically change the situation.

It is such a blatant contradiction to God's purpose that Holy Spirit baptism makes us "joint-heirs with Christ," to the promises of God, and yet in practice, Black Pentecostals remain separate from and unequal to White Pentecostals. Dr. Leonard Lovett, a Black Pentecostal scholar, recently stated, "It is much easier to reject than to refute the fact that racial reconciliation within the Pentecostal Movement is nowhere near realization in our time" (Lovett 1996, 3).

In 1948, the Pentecostal Fellowship of North America (PFNA) was formed with Blacks and other non-Whites formally and officially excluded from membership. That practice continued until 1994. In October of that year, the PFNA convened in Memphis, Tennessee, at which time its leadership announced publicly that it had been a racist organization throughout its 46-year history. The PFNA was then dissolved voluntarily and a new organization, the Pentecostal/Charismatic Churches of North America (PCCNA), was established in its place.

A new governing board was elected consisting of six Whites and six African-Americans. Bishop Ithiel Cleamons of the Church of God in Christ, an African-American, was elected as the first chairperson, and Bishop Barbara Amos of the Mt. Sinai Holy Church of America became the lone female board member. Although many consider this a great accomplishment—and it was—two obvious sins were committed by conference organizers. The first was that they refused to invite Hispanic-Americans and other non-white Pentecostals to participate in the Memphis dialogue. Moreover, and in keeping with a long-standing tradition, Oneness Pentecostals were also excluded from the Memphis conference on the grounds that they were still considered the "theological stepchildren" of the Pentecostal Movement.

Almost all of the 200 delegates at the Memphis conference were men. And although Bishop Barbara Amos was elected to the new governing board, even she could not escape the wrath of this "all boys" network. Some of the men in attendance refused to pray and to dialogue with a woman present in the room. This is a clear indication that the main agenda item at Memphis was race relations between Black and White males. The need to eliminate discrimination against women and other minority groups was not foremost in the minds of conference planners.

The Memphis conference has been given mixed reviews. And though this latest attempt to secure greater racial reconciliation was far from perfect, most observers feel that the efforts of the PCCNA should be continued with a spirit of cautious optimism.

Racial attitudes among Black Pentecostals are no better than those of Whites. Generations of racism have created such a lingering distrust among Blacks that many of us are, for the most part, neutral about a desire for racial harmony within the movement. Hispanic-Americans, other non-whites, and women are frequently left to sit on the sidelines of any discussions regarding reconciliation. It is as though they do not even exist. And in the midst of this spirit of separatism and sin, we still dare to utter the words, "Even so, come Lord Jesus."

Unitarian/Trinitarian Debate

The debate between Oneness and Trinitarian Pentecostals revolves around two main points: (1) the Unitarian or Triune nature of God, and (2) whether or not a person is saved if he/she has not submitted to water baptism in the name of Jesus only. The proponents on either side of this long-standing argument are firmly entrenched in their respective camps, and the Unitarian/Trinitarian debate continues to tear away at the solidarity of the Pentecostal Movement.

Since 1914, Trinitarian and Oneness (Unitarian) Pentecostals have engaged in a continual attack and counterattack struggle, each insisting that the other is theologically wrong and, therefore, living in sin. Unitarians, representing one-fourth (25 percent) of all Pentecostals, have generally been labeled as a group who labors under an illusion of who God actually is. For example, it was mentioned in Chapter 4 that Oneness Pentecostals idenitify Christ as the "sum of God" who performs all the functions of the Father, the Son, and the

Holy Spirit by Himself. Christ alone is God, and beside Him there is no other. The current chapter, rather than continuing the argument for or against the Oneness doctrine, addresses the fact that the Unitarian/Trinitarian debate erodes the spirit of unity within the Pentecostal family.

Gregory A. Boyd has offered an analysis and critique of the Oneness doctrine in his book, *Oneness Pentecostals and The Trinity* (Boyd, 1992). Boyd, "a former Oneness Pentecostal," has presented a scholarly and compelling argument in which he attempts to refute many Oneness claims. Although Dr. Boyd takes a disciplined approach to his writing, I regret that the first book on Oneness Pentecostalism offered by a major publisher was authored by a man who not only disagrees with the Oneness doctrine, but who, in fact, considers it to be sub-Christian in content. In typical Pentecostal fashion, Boyd offers that a part of his ministry includes rescuing other Unitarians from the error of their theological ways.

On the other side of the ledger, Oneness proponents have contended that Trinitarians, especially those who have not been baptized in Jesus' name or spoken in tongues, are not really saved. As I was growing up within the Oneness tradition it was always our hope that Trinitarians would someday denounce their belief in the Trinitarian theories of the third century and return to their Bible-based home of Oneness Pentecostalism.

I have worshiped and worked closely with both Oneness and Trinitarian Pentecostals for many years, and on the surface, this debate appears to be a simple doctrinal disagreement. But at its root is a divisive spirit that encourages brothers and sisters in Christ to discredit the validity of one another's fellowship with God. This is an extremely dangerous position to take regardless of who is scripturally correct.

It is my prayer that leaders on both sides of the Unitarian/Trinitarian issue will seek to understand the common ground that they occupy in the Kingdom of God. In doing so, they will undoubtedly be helping to close the ranks within God's advancing army.

Misrepresentation of Pentecostal Authority:
The Use of Jesus' Name

The final issue to be addressed in this chapter is the question of the correct perception of the Pentecostal's authority in the Kingdom of God. A trademark of Pentecostal believers, in fact, of all evangelical faithfuls, is our insistence upon injecting the name of Jesus into our prayers and into our everyday lives. This is not a matter of habit or convenience, but it is a regular part of our daily routine. For Pentecostals, there can be no Christianity without the living Christ. We need to understand the significance of this tradition, particularly in light of many modern-day abuses.

Since the Azusa Street Revivals, a quiet yet fervent debate has continued regarding the use of Jesus' name as a relevant theme within the Pentecostal culture. Some have questioned whether it is necessary at all, yet others have found its usage expedient, though not essential to the normative work of God's Kingdom. For instance, many early Pentecostals insisted that the name of Jesus be used in the ritual of water baptism. But today, some Trinitarian and many non-denominational Pentecostals see the issue of invoking Jesus' name in water baptism as a matter of personal preference.

Jesus, nearing the end of His earthly ministry, wanted to encourage His followers to go forward with the campaign to preach the gospel. He promised them that the Holy Spirit would come to empower and to uplift them in their efforts. He also informed them that His impending crucifixion would gain for them a measure of entitlement with the Father that they had not previously known.

On one occasion, Jesus told His disciples, "...He that believeth on Me, the works that I do shall he do also; and greater works than these shall he do; because I go unto My Father" (Jn. 14:12). Later, He promised them, "...ye shall receive power, after that the Holy Ghost is come upon you: and ye shall be witnesses unto Me..." (Acts 1:8). In other words, the Holy Spirit would empower them to live and to act like Christ.

Jesus performed many miracles, operating under the anointing of the Holy Spirit and on the strength of His own intimate position with the Father. He restored sight to the blind, and He fed the hungry. By His hand, people were raised from the dead and healed of various diseases. But Jesus also effected a transfer of power from Himself to those who would continue to promote His teachings after He was gone.

Following Jesus' resurrection and ascension to the Father, His disciples began to perform many miracles, operating in the power of the Holy Spirit. On one occasion, apostles Peter and John encountered a lame man at the entrance to the temple where they went for worship. As the man begged alms of them, Peter said, "...Look on us" (Acts 3:4). Peter then added, "...Silver and gold have I none; but such as I have give I thee: In the name of Jesus Christ of Nazareth rise up and walk" (Acts 3:6). The man, who had been afflicted since birth, was healed instantly and began to leap and rejoice. When a crowd of onlookers began to question, Peter preached to them about Jesus and offered that "...His [Jesus'] name through faith in His name hath made this man strong..." (Acts 3:16).

Later, at a Jewish inquiry, Peter said of Jesus, "Neither is there salvation in any other: for there is none other name under heaven given among men whereby we must be saved" (Acts 4:12). In these two instances it was shown that the name of Jesus was effective both for healing and for salvation. A real transfer of power from Christ to His disciples had, in fact, taken place.

The phrase, "in the name of Jesus," literally means in the authority that Jesus alone has with the Father. Jesus said that He is the door through which we must pass in order to gain access to the Father (see Jn. 14:6). When we invoke His name, we acknowledge that He has paid the ultimate price for our salvation, a payment without which we would be alienated from God. We are, therefore, giving honor to Him who makes it possible for us to be heard in the throne room of Heaven. The power is in His blood, but the authority is in His name, the name of Jesus.

Human Error and Abuse

Many people, myself included, have used the phrase, "in the name of Jesus," as one would rub a rabbit's foot or throw salt over a shoulder. Applied in this manner, the phrase becomes nothing more than a Christian lucky charm, a fetish to be worshiped instead of God.

A few years ago, I watched a televised professional boxing match. One of the combatants said in a pre-fight interview that he had prayed in Jesus' name and had been given assurance that he would win. He subsequently entered the ring and lost the fight.

A friend of mine once prayed in Jesus' name that a particular gentleman in whom she was interested would become her husband. Certain that her prayer had been answered, she began to publicly announce her future marriage. Sure enough, within a few months, the gentleman in question proudly announced his engagement. But to my friend's dismay, the man selected another woman as his bride.

When we go into the presence of God representing ourselves or seeking to meet our own selfish needs, we enter as thieves and renegades. Should we approach the Father in this manner, we will have no influence with Him because Christ is not interceding for us. We have a responsibility to check our motives before we approach God with our requests. There is a need for much prayerful instruction and guidance in this area.

The question of the integrity of Christ's name has been quite prevalent, even since the days of the early Church. The case is recorded in the Book of Acts concerning the attempted exorcism of a demon-possessed man by seven sons of a Jewish priest. These young zealots had witnessed many miracles that God had performed through the apostle Paul. Intrigued by Paul's pattern of invoking the name of Jesus, they were anxious to try out this method in their exorcism efforts. They spoke to the demon spirit in the man, saying, "We adjure [command] you by Jesus whom Paul preacheth" (Acts 19:13b).

The evil spirit, who would have been powerless against Jesus, was also subject to Paul's authority. But he was not afraid of these youths, even though the odds were seven-to-one in their favor. He spoke from within the man, saying, "Jesus I know, and Paul I know, but who are ye?" (Acts 19:15b) According to Scripture, the evil spirit then left the man and "...leaped on them, and overcame them, and prevailed against them, so that they fled out of that house naked and wounded" (Acts 19:16).

The forces of hell are not afraid of us just because we pray in the name of Jesus. They only fear and respond to the life of Jesus that is manifested within us. Hence, an important Kingdom principle is this: *We may operate in the power of Christ to the extent that we live in subjection to His authority.*

Everyone who prays in the name of Jesus is not self-centered and insincere. Most people who engage in this practice are earnestly petitioning God to grant requests that are consistent with various promises in His Word. Praying in Jesus' name is necessary. There is plenty of scriptural evidence to support the fact that the prayer of faith influences Heaven and changes things on the earth. Paul's statement in the Book of Colossians is clear that not only with prayer, but "...whatsoever ye do in word or deed, do all in the name of the Lord Jesus, giving thanks to God and the Father by Him" (Col. 3:17). But when we invoke the name of Jesus, we must bow to His authority and preeminence in our lives. For, unless He intercedes for us with the Father, we will have no audience in Heaven.

The Sovereignty of God Beyond Our Faith

Each time we receive a positive answer to prayer or God performs a miracle for us, it increases our belief that we have a close relationship with Him. But there are occasions when, after we have prayed and have believed God, we get either the wrong answer or we get no answer at all. It is as though God has somehow forgotten us. It is at these times that God challenges us to trust Him even more. It may be unpopular to talk about these instances, but they do occur.

A few years ago, I was part of a group of several hundred people who prayed for a woman who was seriously ill. As we prayed in Jesus' name for her healing, we were filled with faith and were confident that our petitions had touched the heart of God. Within a few days, however, the woman died. Many in the prayer group were devastated and confused, asking why God apparently did not honor His Word. Some thought that perhaps we had failed to work the right combination that would unlock and release this particular blessing. Others thought that God had ignored us completely. One experienced and wise believer reminded us that beyond our faith—beyond what we desired—was a God who was sovereign at all times.

Yes, God is sovereign, which means that He has the final word in all issues. His ways and thoughts differ from ours (see Is. 55:8). Therefore, His decisions and actions will frequently be in opposition to our finite expectations. He will continue to have the last word in everything. Does this mean, then, that the only politically correct prayer is, "God, if it be Thy will"? Does the concept of faith only apply within the pages of the Bible? Are miracles a thing of the past? The answer to all these questions is "no!" Our responsibility is to continue to believe, trust, and obey God.

We will see more answers to prayer. We will receive more miracles. But God is neither employed by us, nor is He answerable to us in any way. Too often we, as Pentecostals, have fallen into the trap of trying to force God to fit into our limited perspective of who He is and what He should do. This, along with the other misconception that we are the only true believers, must be passionately avoided, even resisted, if we are to become fruitful stewards in God's Kingdom.

Michael Dusing has offered a recommendation on how Pentecostals should view the issue of suffering and healing. He presents a realistic and yet faith-filled approach to accepting God's will in all matters:

> "The people of God, whether they lived before or after the Cross event, are not immune to sickness, and do not always receive healing in this life...Suffering, therefore, is not only to be expected

in this life, but may actually be God's will for the immediate situation in a believer's life. Since it is the Lord and not the believer who is in charge, it is he alone who makes the decision to heal or not to heal according to his own sovereign nature and purposes. One can therefore, trust God in all circumstances, for 'he does all things well' " (Dusing 1996, 36-37).

I must say "amen" to that profound spiritual wisdom!

Lord, Teach Us How to Pray

Although we might not realize it, the primary objective of prayer is not to receive some "thing" from God, but rather to engage in comprehensive communication with Him regarding His business. Jesus gave instruction that we should always pray and not be fainthearted (see Lk. 18:1). Paul added simply, "Pray without ceasing" (1 Thess. 5:17). Therefore, although we may not totally understand it, prayer is definitely the way for us to gain immediate and lasting intimacy with God.

We must understand that God's answers to our prayers are always given in the context of who He is and not on the basis of what we want. We can, therefore, lessen the level of our frustration about His responses to us as we become more knowledgeable about the comprehensive nature of prayer. The more we understand and cultivate our prayer life, the more will be the times when our prayers and God's answers will be in direct alignment. After all, as Leonard Ravenhill has said, "Of this let us be sure, the prayer closet is not a place merely to hand the Lord a list of urgent requests. Does prayer change things? Yes, but prayer changes men" (Ravenhill 1991, 154).

Prayer Changes Us

Pentecostalism was not born as the result of a spiritual pep rally. And Pentecostals did not always begin our services with a quick preliminary prayer and Scripture reading, followed by a 45-minute "hype" by the Praise and Worship team. Dr. Cheryl Bridges Johns has offered that:

"Pentecostalism was birthed out of the hungering cries of simple people who desired to see the glory of God. Dead orthodoxy and creedal rigidity had hid the face of God from the humble, the contrite, and the broken. God heard the cries of these people and filled their hearts with His fire" (Bridges Johns 1995, 13-14).

If this is the way that it started, surely, it is the way that it should continue. In their book, *Living and Praying In Jesus' Name*, Dick Eastman and Jack Hayford remind us of how we may best serve Christ and be in partnership with Him. "Seasoned warriors of prayer learn to fight their battles from the throne room of God where we sit together with Christ in heavenly places" (Eastman and Hayford 1988, 131).

As we pray and as we believe, we must understand that God is not capricious. He is not trying to trick us. Furthermore, He is not diminished; He has lost no power. From the beginning to the end, He is sovereign. Although we may never totally understand why God might allow us to suffer, it is clear that He has not exempted Himself from that same process. As Dorothy Sayers points out:

"For whatever reason God chose to make man as he is—limited and suffering and subject to sorrows and death—He had the honesty and courage to take His own medicine. Whatever game He is playing with His creation, He has kept His own rules and played fair. He can exact nothing from man that He has not exacted from Himself. He Himself has gone through the whole of human experience...he was born in poverty and in disgrace and thought it well worthwhile" (see Dusing 1996, 18).

Grief Work

The atmosphere among the 120 believers on the Day of Pentecost was charged with the spirit of unity. There was a singularity of purpose as these sincere hearts awaited the infusion of God's mighty power. We can recapture that unity today, but it will cost us the price of our repentance and inner cleansing before God. Jesus prayed, "...Holy Father, keep through thine own name those whom

Thou hast given Me, that they may be one, as We are" (Jn. 17:11). This certainly should be our prayer as well.

In a timely appeal, Dr. Cheryl Bridges Johns challenges Pentecostals to do "grief work," or as we used to call it, "praying through." Her words carry a prophetic tone:

"If Pentecostals are to respond adequately to the imperial boasts of the day, they must, like Hezekiah, do 'grief work.' Behind the wall of Pentecostal churches there needs to be heard the sounds of lament. Pentecostals too must cry out 'This is a day of distress, of rebuke, and of disgrace, children have come to birth and there is no strength to deliver' " (Bridges Johns 1995, 14).

The above-mentioned suggestion brings back to my mind the memories of the "shut-ins" that we used to have when I was growing up. We would go into the church on a Friday night and stay on our knees until early Sunday morning. We would then go home, get cleaned up, and return for Sunday service. In those days, there were no carpeted floors or padded pews. We brought pillows from home and knelt on them, and when we could stay awake no longer, we slept on them. This may seem like a strange practice but our sole purpose was to reach God. And that we did!

Although some may feel that we have outgrown this type of simple behavior, and although newcomers to the movement may have never participated in such an event, I believe that we are being challenged by God Himself to return to that "Old Landmark." André Crouch, the well-known gospel songwriter, composed a song several years ago entitled, "Take Me Back." I believe that the words of that song hold profound significance for our present circumstance. André wrote: "Take me back, take me back, Dear Lord, to the place where I first received you. Take me back, take me back, Dear Lord, where I first believed."

A part of doing grief work requires that we overcome our pride and that silly modern notion that "real men and women don't cry." For as Bridges Johns states:

"Grief work does not look good on television, sound just right on the radio. Grief work, in expressing sighs and groans too deep to be spoken, is embarrassing to those who claim the language of reasoned discourse. But grief work, like no other, is maturing work. It is maturing because it dares to face the cause of shame and make it public" (Bridges Johns 1995, 14-15).

Modern Pentecostalism is not a man-made invention. And although it has become a growing and varied collection of institutions, it remains a movement of God through which the Holy Spirit stirs human hearts, drawing them to the living Christ.

Baptism in the Holy Spirit is a Pentecostal trademark, a spiritual awakening, in which we are endowed with a specific measure of God's grace subsequent to salvation. Spirit baptism is an immersion into the life of Christ through which we not only exhibit the initial evidentiary sign of speaking in other tongues as the Holy Spirit gives the utterance, but we also become coworkers with Christ in His redemptive mission. Any attempt by anyone to reduce this spiritual process to a legalistic formula undermines its life-changing and dynamic character.

Conclusion

It is no secret that the first 96 years of the Twentieth Century Pentecostal Movement have been a theological, social, and political roller-coaster ride. In charting our future, we have much work to do. We have many issues before us that must be resolved. But we are still here, and we are still growing. This is an exciting time—a time for earnest anticipation of what God is going to do next.

I join the great "cloud of witnesses" who believe that we are yet to see God's greatest outpouring upon humankind. The *Spirit of Pentecost*, the revelation of the fullness of God in Christ and in us, is alive and well. As we operate under the leadership and inspiration of the Holy Spirit, we will fulfill Jesus' charge to be "...witnesses unto Me...unto the uttermost part of the earth" (Acts 1:8). God is not through with us yet. I believe that we will fulfill our ordained purpose, not because we are so creative, but because it is God's will.

Challenge Questions

1. Can a person be filled with and led by the Holy Spirit and still remain a racist and a sexist?
2. Where does the responsibility lie for working to achieve greater unity within the Pentecostal Movement?
3. What steps must be taken in order to resolve the major theological and ideological differences that exist between Pentecostals and other Christians?
4. In addition to the sign of speaking in other tongues, what should we exhibit in order to confirm the validity of Holy Spirit baptism in our lives?
5. What strategies might be employed that would help to bridge the gap between Oneness Pentecostals and the rest of the Pentecostal Movement?

References:

Butler, Anthea. "Walls of Division: Racism's Role in Pentecostal History," a paper presented at the Twenty-Fourth Annual Meeting of the Society for Pentecostal Studies, Wheaton College, Wheaton, IL: November 10-12, 1994.

Boyd, Gregory A. *Oneness Pentecostals and the Trinity*. Grand Rapids, MI: Baker Book House, 1992.

Burgess, Stanley M., Gary B. McGee, and Patrick H. Alexander, eds. *Dictionary of Pentecostal and Charismatic Movements*. Grand Rapids, MI: Zondervan Publishing House, 1988.

Dayton, Donald. *Theological Roots of Pentecostalism*. Metuchen, NJ and London: The Scarecrow Press, 1987.

Dusing, Michael. "Toward a Pentecostal Physical Suffering," a paper presented at the Twenty-Fifth Annual Meeting of the Society for Pentecostal Studies, Toronto, Ontario, Canada: March 7-9, 1996.

Eastman, Dick, and Jack Hayford. *Living and Praying in Jesus' Name*. Wheaton, IL: Tyndale House Publisher, Inc., 1988.

Johns, Cheryl Bridges. "The Adolescence of Pentecostalism: In Search of a Legitimate Secterian Society," *PNEUMA: The Journal of the Society for Pentecostal Studies*, 17:1, Spring 1995: 3-17.

Lovett, Leonard. "Looking Backward to Go Forward," a paper presented at the Twenty-Fifth Annual Meeting of the Society for Pentecostal Studies, Toronto, Ontario, Canada: March 7-9, 1996:1-4.

McDonnell, Kilian. "Improbable Conversation: The International Classical Pentecostal/Roman Catholic Dialogue," *PNEUMA: The Journal of the Society for Pentecostal Studies*, 17:2, Fall 1995: 163-188.

Ravenhill, Leonard. *Why Revival Tarries*. Mineapolis, MN: Bethany House Publishers, 1959.

Robeck, Cecil M., Jr. "Taking Stock of Pentecostalism: The Personal Reflections of a Retiring Editor," *PNEUMA: The Journal of the Society for Pentecostal Studies*, 15:1, Spring 1993:35-60.

Part 4

Advancing the Kingdom of God

Wherefore take unto you the whole armour of God, that ye may be able to withstand in the evil day, and having done all, to stand (Ephesians 6:13).

Chapter 8

The Glory of the Latter House

The glory of this latter house shall be greater than of the former, saith the Lord of hosts: and in this place will I give peace, saith the Lord of hosts (Haggai 2:9).

We Will Make It

Much space has been given in the last several chapters to an examination of the fallibility and apparent weakness of the Pentecostal Movement. It should be clear that most of what is wrong is less a matter of the inadequacy of the Pentecostal experience and belief than it is of our refusal to be led by the Holy Spirit.

The time has come for us to begin the work of rebuilding the "broken walls of Pentecostalism." But where does such a work begin? What parts of the walls are broken, and where do repairs need to be made? God's people have been at this place before, and He had an answer for them, just as He has for us. As we try to recover our former glory, we once again consult Israel's experience.

In 536 B.C., the first Jewish exiles returned to Palestine from Babylonian captivity under Zerubbabel. One of God's first assignments was to rebuild the temple. They completed laying the foundation and then, as result of interference from outside rulers and their own lack of interest, the project was stopped. As the Israelites became increasingly preoccupied with rebuilding their own communities, something went wrong. It seemed that the more they toiled, the less they had to show for it. For some reason, they were struggling to meet their most basic survival needs. As they searched to find an answer to their dilemma, God spoke through Haggai, saying: "...Consider your ways" (Hag. 1:7). The Israelites had misplaced their priorities, forsaking the work of God and the rebuilding of His temple, in favor of their own survival activities.

God commissioned Haggai to explain to His people the reason for their failing economy:

> *Ye looked for much, and, lo, it came to little; and when ye brought it home, I did blow upon it. Why? saith the Lord of hosts. Because of Mine house that is waste, and ye run every man unto his own house* (Haggai 1:9).

Haggai encouraged the nation to rededicate themselves to their assigned task, and he reminded them that as a result of their faithfulness, God would prosper them in a greater way than ever before (see Hag. 2:9).

As we approach the twenty-first century, the modern Pentecostal harvest is smaller than it should be, not because Pentecostalism is irrelevant or because our marketing strategies are inadequate. Rather, God has "blown" on many of our efforts so that we might *consider our ways*. I believe that we, too, can reap a great harvest. We can see God's glory increased within us as we ignore all outside influences, turn away from the self-centeredness of our own denominations, doctrines, and creeds, and pursue the fulfillment of our purpose in God.

God Has a Purpose

God has a purpose for each of us. He works within us, for us, and through us in bringing that purpose to a complete reality. And He does not stop short of His expectation just because we change our minds or we become involved in something that we consider more important.

God's work within us is designed so that we might be conformed to the standard of His image and likeness. Paul said, "But we all, with open face beholding as in a glass the glory of the Lord, are changed into the same image from glory to glory, even as by the Spirit of the Lord" (2 Cor. 3:18). God is constantly challenging us to examine ourselves in the light of His holy standard. He does not presume that we are already perfect, walking through life in a sterile state of sinless purity. He requires, instead, that we present ourselves to Him—spirit, mind, and body—desiring to be developed and matured after His pattern (see Rom. 12:1-2).

God seasons us daily with the elements of His character so that we may become the finished product of His hand. "For it is God which worketh in you both to will and to do of His good pleasure" (Phil. 2:13).

Moreover, God clears a path for us so that we may walk in the realization of His grace. Our giftings, our personalities, and the events that shape us are designed with God's purpose in mind. The Psalmist said, "The steps of a good man are ordered by the Lord: and He delighteth in his way" (Ps. 37:23). Who is good, and by what standards is that goodness measured? Whatever positive qualities we have come from Almighty God, and He alone is the righteous Judge.

God orders our lives, and He makes no mistakes. If something appears to go wrong, He knows how to adjust for it. Our successes and failures perform the same function—to make us complete in Him.

Finally, God's dealings within us and for us occur in order that His will may be accomplished through us. Our challenge is to know that, "...the Lord thy God, He is God, the faithful God, which keepeth covenant and mercy with them that love Him and keep His commandments to a thousand generations" (Deut. 7:9). Who is He faithful to, if not to us who believe and trust Him?

We have been created and preordained to play a major role in the fulfillment of God's vision and purpose. His dreams and plans for this universe have a human component. We should not think it strange, therefore, when He chooses to work through us. Rather, we should be concerned if He does not. I, for one, want to be included in His plans.

It Is Finished

Jesus prayed to the Father just prior to His arrest by Roman soldiers on the charge of blasphemy. Seeing the impending reality of

Calvary's cross, Jesus said, "...Father, the hour is come; glorify Thy Son, that Thy Son also may glorify Thee" (Jn. 17:1). Confident that He had been obedient to the Father, Jesus continued:

I have glorified Thee on the earth: I have finished the work which Thou gavest Me to do. And now, O Father, glorify Thou Me with Thine own self with the glory which I had with Thee before the world was (John 17:4-5).

Within days, Jesus was falsely accused, wrongly convicted, and His body affixed to a cross between two thieves. He had submitted to the vigilante justice of an accusing mob. Now He was being pierced and wounded.

As Jesus hung suspended between Heaven and hell, as nails were driven into His hands and feet, He gave Himself as a ransom for the sins of the world. Before His last breath, He told the world what He had already told the Father: "...It is finished..." (Jn. 19:30). Were these the vain utterances of an impostor whose mission had failed? Absolutely not. In fact, they were clearly the words of a triumphant victor.

Jesus knew that He had come to bring salvation into the world. He also remembered that in the Garden of Eden, in the midst of man's darkest hour, God had pronounced that Jesus, the "seed of the woman," would strike the fatal blow to the head [authority] of satan (see Gen. 3:15). Jesus was fully aware that He must fulfill the prophecy of Isaiah, who had pronounced that Christ would "...swallow up death in victory..." (Is. 25:8). He knew that His was the only sacrifice acceptable for restoring humankind to right-standing with God. And so it was that Jesus, the Son of God, died in apparent disgrace and defeat. But the story did not end there.

Three days following His burial, Jesus was resurrected and proceeded to a Galilean hillside where He proclaimed, "All power is given unto Me in heaven and in earth" (Mt. 28:18b). The apostle Paul said that as a result of Jesus' complete sacrifice,

...God also hath highly exalted Him, and given Him a name which is above every name: that at the name of Jesus every knee should bow, of things in heaven, and things in earth and things

under the earth, and that every tongue should confess that Jesus Christ is Lord, to the glory of God the Father (Philippians 2:9-11).

Thereafter, all who would believe on Jesus as Savior and Lord would receive the free gift of salvation and eternal life.

Humankind would no longer be required to offer an external sacrifice for sin, Jesus having paid the sin-debt in full. No one could be excluded from having intimate fellowship with God, except through a conscious decision to reject Christ. No race or class of people would be considered above another. All would have free access to the Father through Christ, who said,

Come unto Me, all ye that labour and are heavy laden, and I will give you rest. Take My yoke upon you, and learn of Me; for I am meek and lowly in heart: and ye shall find rest unto your souls (Matthew 11:28-29).

This invitation stands today as a valid commitment from Christ that He will be our haven of safety in this age and in the ages to come. Because He has not given up, neither can we. But there is more.

Jesus said, "And this gospel of the kingdom shall be preached in all the world for a witness unto all nations; and then [not before] shall the end come" (Mt. 24:14). There is much work yet to be done. So, we need to ready ourselves. God's work through the Church will be more fruitful during the last days than in previous times.

Already, but Not Yet

Much of Pentecostal teaching emphasizes the belief that the future largely determines the present. Therefore, whatever God has promised for the world, the Church, and unbelievers must come to pass. We are living each day in the reality of an "already, but not yet" existence. We have already won in the spirit, though we still war in the flesh. We are now seated in heavenly places in Christ Jesus (see Eph. 2:6), while we yet live on this earth.

The Pentecostal world view is based upon our "already, but not yet" position in Christ. The apostle John, explaining what it means to live in the present hope of a future reality, said, "Beloved, now [already] are we the sons [and daughters] of God, and it doth not yet appear what we shall be: but we know that, when He [Christ] shall appear, we shall be like Him; for we shall see Him as he is" (1 Jn. 3:2).

The blood of Jesus, the sinless Lamb of God, has been offered as complete payment for the total offense of humankind against God. That payment is made operational in us through our ongoing confession of the Lordship of Christ and our willingness to serve God. John said, "...and this is the victory that overcometh the world, even our faith. Who is he that overcometh the world, but he that believeth that Jesus is the Son of God?" (1 Jn. 5:4-5)

But how can we demonstrate that we are on the winning side when it often appears that we are losing? How can we prove to the world that living for Christ is the only way to be truly successful? And what are the attributes of those who will live and walk in victory during these last days?

Portrait of God's Overcomers

God's "end-time overcomers" must meet several requirements. First, we must develop *experience-based fellowship with God*. Our comprehensive knowledge of God will enhance our belief that His glory will be revealed in us, as long as we stay faithful to Him. We must be convinced that, "...the sufferings of this present time are not worthy to be compared with the glory which shall be revealed in us" (Rom. 8:18). We may have setbacks. We may suffer personal losses. But we will know that, "...in all these things we are more than conquerors through Him that loved us" (Rom. 8:37). Therefore, none of our setbacks or losses can defeat us.

Second, we must be committed to a *Bible-based lifestyle*. In other words, we must have a biblical world view, and everything we do must be based upon that perspective. Although there can be no fanaticism or cultishness among us, we must believe and live in obedience to the Word of God. Even before we are born again, satan lives in fear of that day when we discover that our lives are not our own and that we have been bought with the price of Christ's blood.

We will not all become religious professionals, but we all must develop a priority system that makes everything else secondary to what God wants. Our will must become enveloped into God's will, as revealed within His Word. As a result, we will become selfish about how we spend our time and energy. Everything outside of God's purpose will be seen as a luxury that we cannot afford.

God's overcomers meet a third requirement in that we have a *profound understanding of the Kingdom of God*, what it is, and how it operates to achieve His desires. It will be easier, therefore, for us to yield to God's will, for we will understand the consequences of that type of obedience. Every resource—natural, physical, financial, political, and otherwise—is now available to us. We may not have everything we want, but we will have all we need. Instead of spending endless hours begging God to make a way out of no way, we must simply walk in the path He has cleared for us.

Finally, we are required to engage in a constant and unwavering *pursuit of the Kingdom of God*. We must be "sold out" to Him. We must yield to His sovereignty, bow to His Lordship, and walk in the power of His might. We must resist the temptation to take credit for our successes and to seek promotion through political maneuverings. Instead, we must place ourselves in subjection to God's will, knowing that He alone will be glorified. Our responsibility is to consecrate ourselves and live in disciplined obedience to His Word. Whatever deficiencies we have, He will compensate for them.

We may not become wealthy. We may not develop the biggest ministries in our cities. We may not be healed of all our physical ailments before we die. At first glance, we may not appear to be successful at all. But if we decide to sell out to God—if we once exalt Him to the place of complete authority in our hearts—His glory will be revealed from within us, and we will reflect His image, the image of Christ.

Conclusion

God has created us with the capacity to overcome. I am convinced that He wants us to live in complete victory in Him. And as we pursue that vision, we must understand the basic principles that enhance our development in God. The Kingdom, the power, and the glory belong to God (see Mt. 6:13b). He is, therefore, not dependent upon people to be God. But He wants us to acknowledge His preeminence among us. He wants to be King of kings and Lord of lords in our daily existence.

The baptism in the Holy Spirit, although perceived by the uninformed public as being just an ecstatic experience in which one speaks in unknown tongues, is meant to be an infusion of God's life-changing, world-witnessing, abundant life-giving, satan-defeating power. The Spirit's comprehensive work within the Body of Christ should be of critical interest to the people of the Pentecostal faith. After all, it is we who were the first in the present century to receive Spirit baptism.

The final four chapters of this book will be devoted to an in-depth examination of how we can meet the requirements for becoming God's overcomers. We shall look at ways that we can know God, live in His will, and understand and pursue His Kingdom.

Challenge Questions

1. How can one know that he/she is living in compliance with God's purpose for his/her life?
2. In what ways does the "already, but not yet" concept apply to the everyday experience of Pentecostal believers?
3. In the new birth experience, do we receive the nature of Christ in addition to, or instead of our old nature?
4. In what ways does Holy Spirit baptism empower us beyond the level reached through conversion and sanctification alone?
5. At what point in our Christian experience may we be able to say that we are one of "God's overcomers"?

Chapter 9

Know God

He made known His ways unto Moses, His acts unto the children of Israel (Psalm 103:7).

This chapter offers the first of four challenges regarding ways in which we might bring God's glory into a reality on the earth. In the above-mentioned verse, the Psalmist gives a compelling contrast between knowing God intimately and simply knowing about Him. David's words seem to indicate that Moses knew God for who He was, yet Israel only knew Him for what He could do. Moses learned the character of God through a daily walk of faith and experience. And although Israel clearly witnessed the acts of God, they struggled to understand the scope of His motives toward them, as we do today.

The author of the Book of Hebrews, who was also writing to believers, has stated that it is impossible for us to please God, absent the practice of our faith. That same writer has established the necessity of our faith being founded upon God. He has said, "...for he that cometh to God must believe that He is, and that He is a rewarder of them that diligently seek Him" (Heb. 11:6). In other words, an effective and working faith is built upon our knowledge and conviction that God exists and that He desires our greatest good. It is not enough that we alone are convinced. For, even though non-believers throughout the world have a definite need for God, the main instrument for their hearing of His Word is a Church that demonstrates His life and the life of Christ. The apostle Paul posed several questions that bear directly on this point:

How then shall they call on Him in whom they have not believed? and how shall they believe in Him of whom they have not heard? and how shall they hear without a preacher? And how shall they preach, except they be sent? (Romans 10:14-15a).

It is clear that having faith in God is a requirement for all. But it is also true that we cannot practice faith in a God whom we do not know. We must know who God is: His name, His nature, and His character. Further, we need to be familiar with His major attributes and with the ways in which He operates. For this and other important reasons, engaging in biblical scholarship is a helpful activity.

Additionally, operating under the anointing of particular spiritual gifts is a wonderful experience as well. But this alone is inadequate. Although we preach until the Heavens ring and pray until the forces of hell run in fear; no revelation, no ministry, no work for God is more important than developing intimate fellowship with Him. We all live, move, and have our being in God (see Acts 17:28). Our lives are hidden in Him. Our purpose is conceived by Him. Therefore, knowing God is a key ingredient to our success in life.

It was mentioned in Chapter 3 of this text that having an effective relationship with God is the result of consecration, scholarship, and experience. Taking that as a premise for our discussion, we shall begin the present chapter with a summary review of scriptural data regarding the identity of God. We shall then examine the process involved in knowing God, as experienced by Moses, Israel's first national leader. Next, we shall focus upon the Godship of Jesus Christ and the inclusive significance of His name. Finally, we shall meet the Reverend Ernest L. Hardy, a man who is convinced that Moses' God is our God and that He is still alive.

The Nature of God

Throughout Scripture, God has unfolded His identity to us that we might know Him and learn to have complete confidence in Him in all aspects of our lives. Moses said, "In the beginning God created the heaven and the earth" (Gen. 1:1). John said, "In the beginning was the Word, and the Word was with God, and the Word was God" (Jn. 1:1). Therefore, all that there is or ever will be, starts with

God. In the text, *Systematic Theology: a Pentecostal Perspective* (Horton 1994, 120-131), a distinction is made between the constitutional and moral aspects of God (see Fig. 9.1). His constitutional attributes, those that define the essence of His being, are as follows. God is:

- *Eternal* (see Ps. 33:11; 90:2; Is. 57:15; 1 Tim. 1:17);
- *Knowable* (see Ezek. 20:20; Joel 2:27; Jn. 1:18; Acts 14:17; Rom. 1:18-20);
- *Omniscient* (see Ps. 139:1-4; Is. 40:28; Heb. 4:13);
- *Omnipotent* (see Is. 14:27; 2 Chron. 20:6; Dan. 4:35);
- *Omnipresent* (see Ps. 139:7-10; Jer. 23:24);
- *Spirit* (see Jn. 4:24: 1 Tim. 1:17; 6:16);
- *Wise* (see Dan. 2:21; Ps. 104:24; 147:5).

In addition to His constitutional qualities, God is a moral being. He does not simply possess a set of positive attributes. Rather, these qualities form an integral part of His nature, complete and without measure. God is:

- *Faithful* (see Deut. 7:9; Lam. 3:22-23; Num. 23:19; Heb. 6:17);
- *Good* (see Gen.1:4,10,12, 18, 21, 25, 31; Ps. 100:5; 145:8-9; Lam. 3:25; Acts 14:17; Jas. 1:5);
- *Gracious and Merciful* (see Ex. 22:27; Neh. 9:17,31: Jon. 4:2);
- *Holy* (see Lev. 11:44);
- *Love* (see 1 Jn. 4:8-10; Eph. 2:4);
- *Patient* (see Rom. 2:4; 9:22-23; 2 Pet. 3:9);
- *Righteous and Just* (see Ps. 72:2; 89:14; Deut. 7:9-10; 32:4; 2 Cor. 5:21; 2 Pet. 1:1);
- *Truthful* (see Ps. 33:4; 119:151,160; Is. 55:10-11).

The Redemptive Names of God

The name *YHWH* (*Yahweh*: vowels added) is the most frequent name for God in the Bible, appearing over 6,800 times in the Old Testament alone. The name *Yahweh* literally means, "I Am/I Will Be." It indicates that God is a self-proclaimed and independent being who is the source for all that is and who operates at His own bidding on behalf of His creation.

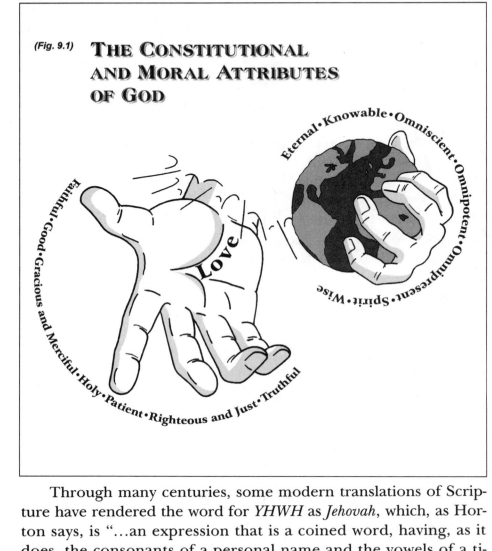

(Fig. 9.1) THE CONSTITUTIONAL AND MORAL ATTRIBUTES OF GOD

Through many centuries, some modern translations of Scripture have rendered the word for *YHWH* as *Jehovah*, which, as Horton says, is "...an expression that is a coined word, having, as it does, the consonants of a personal name and the vowels of a title" (Horton 1994, 135). Therefore, the word *Jehovah* is not the actual name of God. Rather, it is a useful tool for our linguistic convenience.

The following names for God are also revealed in the Old Testament:

- *Adonai*: A Hebrew word for *Master* or *Lord* (see Gen. 15:1,2);
- *Elohim*: God who is complete; plurality (see Gen. 1:1,26; Ps. 68:1);
- *'El 'Elohe Yisra'el*: God, the God of Israel (see Gen. 33:20);
- *'El Elyon*: The most high God (see Gen. 14:22; Num. 14:16; Deut. 32:8);
- *'El 'Olam*: The eternal God (see Gen. 21:33; Ps. 90:2);
- *'El Ro'i*: The God who sees (see Gen. 16:13);
- *'El Shaddai*: The Almighty God; the all-sufficient One (see Gen. 17:1; Ps. 68:14; Is. 13:6; Gen. 48:3-4);
- *Yahweh-nissi*: The Lord is our Banner, or Victor (see Ex. 17:15; Num. 21:8-9; Is. 62:10-11);
- *Yahweh-'osenu*: The Lord is our Maker (see Ps. 95:6);
- *Yahweh-ro'i*: The Lord is my Shepherd (see Ps. 23:1);
- *Yahweh-roph'eka*: The Lord who is Physician and Healer (see Ex. 15:26);
- *Yahweh-sabaoth*: The Lord of Hosts (see Ps. 148:2; Mt. 26:53);
- *Yahweh-Shalom*: The Lord is Peace (see Judg. 6:23);
- *Yahweh-Shammah*: The Lord is there (everywhere): (see Ezek. 48:35);
- *Yahweh-tsidkenu*: The Lord is our Righteousness (see Jer. 23:6; 33:16);
- *Yahweh-yireh*: The Lord will provide (see Gen. 22:14).

It must be noted that the above are not just convenient synonyms to be used in place of the name of God. Rather, through them we are given a progressive revelation of the convergence of the *who* and the *what* of God (see Fig. 9.2). In a word, God is awesome!

The Unity of God

Through Moses, we are told, "Hear, O Israel: The Lord our God is one Lord" (Deut. 6:4). God has always revealed Himself, not as three, but as one. Throughout the New Testament, God is revealed as *Father* (see Jn. 8:54; 20:17); *Son* (see Phil. 2:5-7; Heb. 1:8); and *Holy Spirit* (see Acts 5:3-4; 1 Cor. 3:16). God is One.

(Fig. 9.2) THE REDEMPTIVE NAMES OF GOD

Adonai: A Hebrew Word for Master or Lord

Elohim: God who is complete; plurality

'El Elohe Yisra'el: God, The God of Israel

'El Elyon: The Most High God

El 'Olam: The Eternal God

'El 'Ro'i: The God who sees

'El Shaddai: The Almighty God ; The all-sufficient One

Yahweh-nissi: The Lord is our Banner, or Victor

Yahweh-'osenu: The Lord is our Maker

Yahweh-ro'i: The Lord is my Shepherd

In the Orthodox Christian (and Pentecostal) view, The Father is God, Jesus is God, and the Holy Spirit is God. They are three persons separately who comprise one supreme Individual. This affirmation, in effect since early in the third century A.D., denies the view that God is one person who manifests Himself separately as

Father, Son, and Holy Spirit (Sabellianism). Neither does it support the notion that there are three separate Gods, with the Father serving as the Commander-in-Chief in Heaven and with Jesus and the Holy Spirit each occupying a position of succeedingly lesser authority (Arianism).

Because there has been no accurate replica of God on the earth, except for Christ, it is impossible for the human intellect to satisfactorily explain this spiritual prototype. The following represents an accurate summary of God's coordinated functioning:

> "God the Father is principally credited with the work of the creation; God the Son is the principle agent in applying the work of redemption to humanity; God the Holy Spirit is the deposit, or first installment, guaranteeing our future inheritance" (Menzies and Horton 1994, 54).

At first glance, this delineation appears to indicate that there is a sharp division of labor in the Godhead. Such is not the case. Instead, there exists complete integration, interdependence, and co-equality in all aspects of divine authority throughout eternity—past, present, and future. For as Moses has said, "Before the mountains were brought forth, or ever Thou hadst formed the earth and the world, even from everlasting to everlasting, Thou art God" (Ps. 90:2).

The Father is God completely, and yet, no more so than is Christ or the Holy Spirit. Jesus, in recognizing the functional pre-eminence of the Father, saw Himself as having proceeded forth as God's only begotten Son (see Ps. 2:7; Jn. 3:16; Acts 13:33; Heb. 1:5-6).

Jesus Christ is the living, full, and complete manifestation of God (see Col. 1:9; Jn. 1:14). He is also completely human, yet He is without the sinful nature of man. As a man, He is totally qualified to represent all human beings in the courts of heavenly justice. His task was that of sacrificing His life so that all who were dead in sin might live. As a result of Jesus' death, burial, and resurrection, He has been crowned Lord of all by the Father (see Phil. 2:11). Accordingly, Jesus is Lord because God says so; but He is my Lord because I say so.

Jesus has ascended into Heaven and now occupies the seat of highest authority in the Kingdom of God. I join the untold numbers who look forward with earnest anticipation to His return to the earth when He will finish the work of His calling, which is to bring all nations into fellowship with Him forever.

The Holy Spirit is God. He has all the attributes of God, possessing the definitive character and personality of God, yet He has no physical form. He is the Executor of the New Testament, instructing, enlightening, and convicting us with regard to how we measure up to the standards of Almighty God (see Jn. 14:16-17, 26; 16:7-12). The Holy Spirit abides within us and empowers us to live in accordance with God's will (see Jn. 16:13-15; 20:22; Acts 1:8; 2:4; 8:19).

With an objective and factual description of God, we are privileged to understand what is possible in Him and what we may expect of Him. But there is a significant difference between knowing what is possible and living in the actual experience of something. Although God has revealed Himself to us in both invisible (Spirit) and visible (Christ) form, we are constantly being exposed to a greater level of His self-revelation.

Knowing God denotes a discerning of His life and a sharing with His purpose, rather than just being aware of His Person. This benefit, to which we are entitled, is totally based upon and is the result of our commitment to God's will. In addition, knowing God is not just a fact, but a process as well. We can only know God as Banner, Healer, Peacemaker, Savior, etc., as He is revealed to us on a daily basis. We may experience these realities in our own lives, or vicariously, as they are manifested in others. The purpose for our learning is to know God in His fullness so that the world might know Him as He is revealed through us. Let us examine the experience of Moses, a man with whom God spoke: "...face to face, as a man speaketh unto his friend" (Ex. 33:11a).

Background

When Moses was born, Israel as a nation was in servitude in Egypt. The Egyptian Pharaoh, fearing the political and military implications of a growing Hebrew population, decreed that all male babies born in Israelite households be killed. But before that decree and before time began, God had a vision. His vision was that His entire creation would function in total harmony with Him.

The word *vision*, as seen from the human perspective, is generally used to describe something about which one dreams and fantasizes. It often inludes one's wishes. In the eyes of God, however, vision includes all that He has ordained and, therefore, must come to pass. Note an example.

When God created both male and female in the image and likeness of Himself, His intention was that we would serve and glorify Him throughout all ages. And when Adam and Eve violated God's law, plunging all of us into the abyss of sin and death, it appeared as though God's plan had failed. But when He has a vision, He backs it up with a promise. And each promise is accompanied by a plan for its fulfillment. Therefore, in the midst of man's darkest moment, God made a promise to Himself. In the Garden of Eden, and in the presence of man and satan, God promised that His *Righteous Seed* would literally crush the head (authority) of satan (see Gen. 3:15).

Later on, God found an idol-worshiper by the name of Abram, converted him, and changed his name to Abraham. He entered into a covenant with Abraham and promised that the Righteous Seed of God would come through Abraham's loins (the nation of Israel). God further promised that Abraham's descendants would inherit the land of Canaan forever (see Gen.13:15). Now, there was no nation of Israel in the Garden of Eden. And Pharaoh had not yet been born when God cut covenant with Abraham. But by the time Pharaoh arrived on the scene and issued his decree against the Israelites, their destiny had already been set. For God had spoken.

God Had Spoken

Many do not believe it, but when God speaks, all of creation listens. That law was established long before the world began. And it manifested itself at the time of creation, when God said "...Let there be..." and it was so (see Gen. 1).

God is God alone, and none, therefore, can preclude Him. Pharaoh, Haman, and Herod all failed to defeat Him. Neither Hitler nor Hussein could override Him. The Red Sea was not deep enough, and the Wilderness was not bleak enough. Neither a Jewish exile nor a Holocaust could stop God. And for those who think that the Church today is losing ground, Jesus said, "...and upon this rock I will build My church; and the gates of hell shall not prevail against it" (Mt. 16:18). God's Word is sure.

The Son of Pharaoh's Daughter

Scripture tells us that following Moses' birth, his parents kept him in their home until he was three months old. At that time, his mother placed him in a basket and hid him by the bank of a river, hoping that he would somehow be saved. God had preordained that the baby would be discovered by Pharaoh's daughter. She knew that he was a Hebrew baby; and she knew that according to her father's order, he should be killed. But those facts could not override the God-given compassion that she felt at that moment. She took the child from the hiding place and unwittingly hired Moses' own mother to nurse him for her. "...And she called his name Moses: and she said, Because I drew him out of the water" (Ex. 2:10). From that time on, Pharaoh's daughter raised Moses as her own son.

Although Moses grew up in the Egyptian culture, he was clearly aware that he was an Israelite. He was an adopted son of Pharaoh's daughter, but the blood of his forefathers ran warm within his veins. When he was about 40 years of age, the direction of his life changed drastically. One day, he came upon an Egyptian who was attacking one of his Hebrew countrymen. Moses killed the Egyptian, and when Pharaoh heard about it, he ordered that Moses be brought to justice. Fearing for his life, Moses fled to the land of Midian with a price on his head.

Moses found favor with a Midianite priest and subsequently married his daughter, Zipporah. She bore a son, and Moses named him Gershom, which signified that, "...I have been a stranger in a strange land" (Ex. 2:22). Moses secured a job herding sheep for his father-in-law and seemed content with his new life.

The Call of God

I believe that there were times when Moses' mind would wander. During the warm nights, amidst the bleating of the sheep, his thoughts would turn toward home. He would imagine what might have become of his loving parents and sister who had helped save his life as a baby. I believe that he considered other questions as well. For example, did he have other brothers and sisters? Could he ever go back and live in Egypt? And yes, there were memories of his fellow Hebrews, still in service to the evil Pharaoh.

But nothing about the past could possibly compare with the future that lay ahead, Moses was a man of destiny. His purpose had been divinely established. And although he was not aware of it, the day was soon to come when, on the backside of the desert, he would meet God. Moses was about to be commissioned by God, the Covenant-keeper, to become Israel's first great national leader. Note the following:

And it came to pass in process of time, that the king of Egypt died: and the children of Israel sighed by reason of the bondage, and they cried, and their cry came up unto God by reason of the bondage. And God heard their groaning, and God remembered His covenant with Abraham, with Isaac, and with Jacob. And God looked upon the children of Israel, and God had respect unto them (Exodus 2:23-25).

Moses had spent the first 40 years of his life in Egypt. By our standards, he was already "over the hill." Another 40 years had passed in Midian, and although his life had been fairly prosperous, Moses had done nothing fruitful for God.

One day, while out with his father-in-law's sheep, Moses came upon a mountain. At the top of that mountain he saw a bush that was blazing beneath the glistening sun. He observed the flame, and he felt the intensity of the heat. And although the bush continued to burn, it was not consumed. Moses was investigating the scene when suddenly, he saw the visible form of an angel in the midst of the bush. Startled at first and then amazed, he moved closer.

And when the Lord saw that he turned aside to see, God called unto him out of the midst of the bush, and said, Moses, Moses. And he said, Here am I. And He said, Draw not nigh hither: put off thy shoes from off thy feet, for the place whereon thou standest is holy ground (Exodus 3:4-5).

As a result of his cross-cultural background, Moses had certainly developed a god-concept. Within his Egyptian/Jewish teaching, he had heard about many gods. The Midianites were distant cousins of the Hebrews and descendants of Abraham. So, they, too, were somewhat religious. Therefore, when God informed him that he was now standing on holy ground, Moses knew that he was in the midst of a sacred moment. The same is true for us today. When we come into the presence of God, we need to recognize that we truly are on holy ground.

God introduced Himself in such a manner that it would leave no doubt in Moses' mind regarding His authority. He said, "...I am the God of thy father, the God of Abraham, the God of Isaac, and the God of Jacob" (Ex. 3:6a). At first, Moses was afraid. Not just anyone gets to see a nonconsumable, burning bush and meet God all in the same day. Initially, he could not even lift up his eyes to see the angel of God. Eventually, Moses' fear turned into reverence for this holy God and this holy place.

God informed Moses that he had been chosen as the man who would lead the children of Israel out of Egypt. Forty years earlier, he had saved the life of one Hebrew. His new assignment required him to save an entire nation. Suddenly, Moses' reverence turned into feelings of inadequacy. He said to God, "...Who am I, that I should go unto Pharaoh, and that I should bring forth the children of Israel out of Egypt?" (Ex. 3:11) God assured Moses that He would be with him every step of the way, and He promised Moses complete victory.

Moses still found it difficult to modify his thinking about himself. In his mind, he was still a fugitive from Egyptian justice. It was clear that he needed a major attitude adjustment. Moreover, since he lacked confidence in his own ability, he knew that he must depend on God. But how much of a risk would that be? After 80 years of independent living, he now had a new Boss. In his attempt to validate God's true identity, Moses asked, "...when I come unto the children of Israel, and shall say unto them, The God of your fathers hath sent me unto you; and they shall say to me, What is His name? what shall I say unto them?" (Ex. 3:13) God answered, "...I AM THAT I AM: and He said, Thus shalt thou say unto the children of Israel, I AM hath sent me unto you" (Ex. 3:14). God declared that He alone was the preeminent force in the universe.

"What Is That in Thine Hand?"

God explained to Moses that Pharaoh would initially refuse to allow the Israelites to leave Egypt. But He added, "And I will stretch out My hand, and smite Egypt with all My wonders which I will do in the midst thereof: and after that he will let you go" (Ex. 3:20). But Moses, still hesitating, shifted his attention back to the Israelites. He said, "...But, behold, they will not believe me, nor hearken unto my voice: for they will say, The Lord hath not appeared unto thee" (Ex. 4:1).

It has already been stated that when God speaks, things happen. When He speaks, nothing becomes something. But He knows that people need to see before they will believe, and that actions often speak louder than words alone. It does not matter whether it is Moses who is talking, or a preacher, or you. When words are not enough to get people (or demons) to listen, one must be able to follow up with actions; and those actions must be performed in the authority and power of Almighty God.

In the midst of Moses' self-disqualification, God asked him a simple, probing question: "...What is that in thine hand? [Moses replied], A rod" (Ex. 4:2). Moses could have been referring to his shepherd's staff, or perhaps it was just a stick. But whatever it was, it was enough for God to work with. So, while the rod was still in Moses' hand, God anointed it, and it became "the rod of God..."

(Ex. 4:20b). From that point on, the rod would be a visible symbol of God's anointing upon Moses' life.

Moses made a final plea to be excused from his assignment, offering that he was not eloquent. His statement that he was, "...slow of speech, and of a slow tongue" (Ex. 4:10) did not deter God who was prepared to do with Moses' mouth what He had just done with the rod. Hence, God's response, "...Who hath made man's mouth?...have not I the Lord? Now therefore go, and I will be with thy mouth, and teach thee what thou shalt say" (Ex. 4:11-12). But Moses continued to cry for help. So God agreed to provide Aaron, Moses' brother, as his mouthpiece:

> *...and I will be with thy mouth, and with his mouth, and will teach you what ye shall do. And he shall be thy spokesman unto the people: and he shall be, even he shall be to thee instead of a mouth, and thou shalt be to him instead of God* (Exodus 4:15-16).

God gave a comprehensive plan to Moses:

1. God called Moses and gave him a promise: "...this shall be a token unto thee, that I have sent thee: When thou hast brought forth the people out of Egypt, ye shall serve God upon this mountain" (Ex. 3:12);
2. God ordained Moses and placed him in office: "...and I will send thee unto Pharaoh, that thou mayest bring forth My people the children of Israel out of Egypt" (Ex. 3:10);
3. God gave Moses His anointing: "...this rod in thine hand, wherewith thou shalt do signs" (Ex. 4:17);
4. God educated Moses: "...I will be with thy mouth, and teach thee what thou shalt say" (Ex. 4:12);
5. God gave Aaron as Moses' mouthpiece: "...he shall be to thee instead of a mouth..." (Ex. 4:16).

I believe that the above listing offers a clear way to measure the authenticity of anyone who claims to represent God (see Fig. 9.3). Simply put, he/she will be ordained and anointed by God "to speak and to do signs." In other words, he/she will go forth in the authority and power of God, witnessing verbally for Him and utilizing

God-given abilities to perform His will. This includes demonstrating a lifestyle dedicated to God's holiness.

(Fig. 9.3) **GOD'S GIFTS TO MOSES**

ORDINATION

ANOINTING

MOUTHPIECE

EDUCATION

A PROMISE

   Maintaining intimate fellowship with God is much more important than any ministry or other work that we could perform for Him. In the New Testament, Jesus reminds His followers that it is more important for them to be honored in Heaven than to be feared in hell.

Behold, I give unto you power to tread on serpents and scorpions, and over all the power of the enemy: and nothing shall by any means hurt you. Notwithstanding in this rejoice not, that the spirits are subject unto you; but rather rejoice, because your names are written in heaven (Luke 10:19-20).

But let us return to Moses.

God's Progressive Revelation

Moses agreed to return to Egypt to begin his assignment. He and Aaron appeared before Pharaoh requesting that he release the Israelites. Pharaoh, in an attitude of total defiance, said to them, "...Who is the Lord, that I should obey His voice to let Israel go? I know not the Lord, neither will I let Israel go" (Ex. 5:2). That one phrase, "I know not the Lord," summarizes Pharaoh's ignorance. We can only live in obedience to God if we really know Him. Our obedience may begin in faith, but it grows with our knowledge of and our trust in God.

Pharaoh, instead of yielding to the commandment of God, issued his own command to increase the burden on the Israelites. When Moses complained to God about this, he was told, "...Now shalt thou see what I will do to Pharaoh: for with a strong hand shall he let them go, and with a strong hand shall he drive them out of his land" (Ex. 6:1). God then reiterated something He had told Moses at the site of the burning bush. He said to him, "...I am the Lord: and I appeared unto Abraham, unto Isaac, and unto Jacob, by the name of God Almighty, but by My name JEHOVAH [YHWH] was I not known to them" (Ex. 6:2-3).

The name *Jehovah* is a translation of the name *YHWH*, which we have already determined is the proper name for God throughout the Old Testament. In this situation, God was continuing to reveal Himself to His people. Abraham, Isaac, and Jacob knew God in a sacred and particular way. In fact, Abraham received the original promise to be the father of the Hebrew nation. But God was revealing things about Himself to Moses and to the Israelites that Abraham and the others had not seen.

God Is Faithful to Deliver

In order for God to maintain His integrity, He must honor His word. Such was the case in the deliverance of Israel. God had given

His word and, therefore, it had to come to pass. Because of the disobedience of Pharaoh to His commands, God inflicted ten separate plagues upon the Egyptians, each progressively more severe. Eventually, the angry and frustrated Pharaoh agreed to release God's people. As soon as the words to release the Israelites had left his lips, Pharaoh's heart was hardened toward them. In his anger, he decided to overtake and destroy God's people.

Here we see Moses and the Israelites trying to walk in obedience to God. As they headed toward their Promised Land, they were pursued by the army of Pharaoh. Sandwiched between the Red Sea in front and the Egyptians behind, they were gripped with fear and torment. Four hundred plus years of servitude had produced a slave mentality within the Hebrews that would be difficult for them to overcome.

It is easy for us to criticize the Israelites' apparent lack of faith when we read that God was in control. They actually exhibited a typical human response to the *stuff* of life. Generally, when we encounter pain and suffering, our tendency is to buckle rather than to bristle. Even though we may hear about God's provisions, we are unable to access them. It is at these times that we demonstrate how little we know about God.

Living Faith Works

Moses tried to overcome the fear of the Israelites by encouraging them to,

> *...stand still, and see the salvation of the Lord, which He will show to you today: for the Egyptians whom ye have seen today, ye shall see them again no more for ever. The Lord shall fight for you, and ye shall hold your peace* (Exodus 14:13-14).

Even though Moses was convinced that God would keep His promise, he did not realize the extent to which God was depending on him as a partner. He was just beginning to learn how to remain sensitive to the voice of God in his own life. Even though Moses thought that standing still and watching God work was a sacred thing, as far as God was concerned, a faith that is alive takes action. Therefore, God told him to:

...speak unto the children of Israel, that they go forward: but lift thou up thy rod, and stretch out thine hand over the sea, and divide it: and the children of Israel shall go on dry ground through the midst of the sea (Exodus 14:15-16).

The phrase, "...lift thou up thy rod...", was God's directive for Moses to put his faith to work. There were no engineers who could build a bridge to span the Red Sea. There were no boats available to carry people to the other side. But there was the rod of God in the hands of a man of faith As Moses lifted up the rod, the waters were divided, creating a pathway through which God's people could escape. But as the Israelites were entering this "tunnel of God," the enemy forces were following after them. God then launched His own counter-attack against the Egyptians.

With chariots falling apart and fear building in their hearts, they said to one another, "...Let us flee from the face of Israel; for the Lord fighteth for them against the Egyptians" (Ex. 14:25). It was too late for them to retreat, however. With the Israelites safely on the other side, God commanded Moses once again to stretch the rod toward the sea. As he did so, the parted pillars of water rolled back together on top of Pharaoh and his host. Because of the intervention of God, the Red Sea was transformed from a pathway of salvation into a watery grave. "And Israel saw the great work which the Lord did upon the Egyptians: and the people feared the Lord, and believed the Lord, and His servant Moses" (Ex. 14:31).

Two Different Responses

If we are helped by God and we do not acknowledge that it was He who delivered us, we can totally misrepresent His purpose in our lives. Let us briefly compare Moses' response to God with that of the Israelites.

Immediately following their deliverance from Egypt, the Israelites rejoiced mightily. God entered into a covenant with them, and they seemed ready to progress in Him. God called Moses up to a mountain and instructed him to deliver a message to the nation, designed to solidify their position with Him forever.

Now therefore, if ye will obey My voice indeed, and keep My covenant, then ye shall be a peculiar treasure unto Me above all people: for all the earth is Mine: and ye shall be unto Me a kingdom of priests, and an holy nation...(Exodus 19:5-6).

The people agreed to obey, and all appeared to be going well. God dictated the Ten Commandments to Moses in order that the nation might have clear rules by which to live. But then, at the very moment that God was finalizing His covenant with them, the people began to draw back. Their access to Him at this time was on a restricted basis, and their communication with Him was through Moses. Their concept of God was incomplete and unclear. In their minds, He was really the God of Moses. The man, Moses, was flesh and blood. They could see and talk with him directly. He was more than just their point of contact with God; he was almost God's "personification."

As a result of the mounting apprehension within their minds, the people said to Moses, "...Speak thou with us, and we will hear: but let not God speak with us, lest we die" (Ex. 20:19). Moses tried unsuccessfully to convince them to stay in close fellowship with God. Instead, they: "...stood afar off, and Moses drew near unto the thick darkness where God was" (Ex. 20:21). Moses's interaction with God was intimate. He was "inside the cloud," with the manifested presence of God. He alone experienced that level of closeness.

Here we see God's covenant people running from Him, but Moses was running to Him. They were fearing God at the same time that Moses was bowing before and worshiping Him. As a result, they were blinded to the revelation of God's redemptive purpose in their lives. Having decided to keep their distance from God, the Israelites focused their attention on Moses. And when it appeared that he was spending too much time with God, they created a golden calf to worship, thus replacing both God and Moses. What an unfortunate decision that was! Their fear of God's holiness—of His manifested presence—created a wall of separation between themselves and God, a wall that would remain solid for generations to come.

Unfortunately, the same spirit that limited the ability of God's "elect" of that day to trust Him is still at work today. A prerequisite to our fellowship with God is that we believe and trust Him. Whenever we focus our attention upon a particular person or ideology rather than God, we alienate ourselves from Him.

Show Me Now Thy Way

Moses didn't draw near to God in just some physical place behind a cloud. He drew near in his mind and in his heart. Because of this, God drew close to him. He drew so close in fact, that He could speak to Moses, "...face to face, as a man speaketh unto his friend..." (Ex. 33: 11). It is in this atmosphere of intimate interaction that Moses, the man, dared to approach Almighty God with a most unusual request. "...if I have found grace in Thy sight, show me now Thy way, that I may know Thee, that I may find grace in Thy sight: and consider that this nation is Thy people" (Ex. 33:13). A great transformation had taken place in Moses' life. He was becoming aware that God is comprehensive. He was discovering a new depth in God, and he wanted to pursue that depth of purpose. He wanted to be taken into God's confidence.

Sharing true intimacy with another results from spending quality time together, and Moses knew that he had spent that type of time with God. When Moses was first called to return to Egypt and lead the Israelites out of slavery, he begged God for human help. In response, God provided Aaron. But experience had taught Moses that when the people mutinied against God, Aaron, the human helper, was of no value in fulfilling God's purpose. It was Aaron whose hands had fashioned and constructed the very idol that the people had preferred over God. In the end, Moses wanted neither man nor angel to lead the people. He wanted only God.

What a predictable scenario! The more we walk with God, the more confidence we develop in Him and the less desire we have for substitutes. Moses knew that God was angry with the Israelites for not honoring their commitment to Him. Acting in the role of intercessor, Moses implored God not to abandon him or the people. As

Moses entreated Him, God saw the change in His servant. Speaking with reassurance, God said, "...My presence shall go with thee, and I will give thee rest" (Ex. 33:14). Today, as in the time of Moses, we can rest in the truth that God is with us and in us.

Show Me Thy Glory

Moses, recognizing the intimacy that he was now experiencing with God, pressed on with an even more audacious request. Pushing the envelope of propriety, he implored God, "...I beseech Thee, show me Thy glory" (Ex. 33:18). Here he was, asking God, the I AM, to completely reveal Himself. Moses wanted to gaze directly into the eyes of God. The effect of this experience would have been worse than staring into 10,000 suns. The sheer weightiness of God's holy visage would have been too much for any human to withstand.

That attitude may seem ridiculous to us, but I believe that it pleased God. Recognizing the naive sincerity of Moses, God mercifully informed him, "...Thou canst not see My face: for there shall no man see Me, and live" (Ex. 33:20). Then He added, "...thou shalt see My back parts: but My face shall not be seen" (Ex. 33:23).

In examining the above passage, I have asked myself, "When have I dared to believe God to this point?" My answer is, "I never have." I have not pressed God to the point where He would even consider saying to me, "I am sorry, son, but you are getting a little too close to Me for your own good." That is one of my lifetime goals.

Moses Knew God

Moses' experience could provide a rich study in such topics as developing leadership skills, establishing communications systems, organizing communities, and building management teams. Notwithstanding all of that, the central theme for my study of this outstanding leader is the fact that he knew God. In the beginning of his relationship with God, Moses was no different from anyone else. He had only a basic knowledge of God. During his lifetime, there was no Bible that he could consult in order to understand God's character or method of operation. But Moses was a worshiper and a man with a pliable character. He was willing for God to orchestrate his development slowly and carefully. He was a man of prayer, and he developed an early habit of communing with God.

Some would say that Moses was forced to worship because it was the only way that he could be successful in his mission. Instead, it appears that his disciplined prayer life was motivated more by reverence than by duty. Moses was not seeking a leadership position, but when drafted for service, he approached his responsibility in a serious manner. Although he possessed no extraordinary leadership skills, he walked confidently in his God-given authority. Moses enjoyed a dynamic and progressive relationship with God, and he became a trusted partner in the enterprise of Heaven.

The Revelation of God in Christ

Our discussion to this point has focused upon an Old Testament figure who developed fellowship with the God of the Old Book. One of the major themes within the volume of the New Testament is that God has been incarnated in the person of Jesus Christ.

As we examine the events in Christ's life that are recorded in the four Gospels, we marvel at His miraculous accomplishments, His care for the poor and the infirmed, and His ability to handle the Scriptures. Jesus would have probably met with little resistance had He settled for being a prophet or teacher. These would have caused only minor conflict between Himself and the Jewish leaders of that day. But the main issue around which conflict arose was Christ's claim that He was God's chosen Messiah and Israel's promised King (see Jn. 4:25-26; Mt. 26:63-64; Mk. 14:61-62).

It is recorded in John's Gospel that Jesus was arrested by Roman soldiers and delivered first to Annas, then to Caiaphas, and eventually to Pilate's judgement seat. After questioning Jesus extensively, Pilate could find no law that He had broken that would qualify Him for execution. Pilate questioned the Jews, therefore, concerning their reason for wanting Jesus killed. They replied, "...by our law He ought to die, because He made Himself the Son of God" (Jn. 19:7). When Pilate relented to having Jesus crucified, he had the following title inscribed on Jesus' cross in the Hebrew, Greek, and Latin languages: "JESUS OF NAZARETH THE KING OF THE JEWS" (Jn. 19:19b). The chief priests demanded that Pilate amend the inscription to read, "...He said [claimed that], I am King of the Jews" (Jn. 19:21), but Pilate refused, saying, "...What I have written I have written" (Jn. 19:22). What a revelation on his part!

Jesus: Pentecostalism's Main Figure

Jesus is the central figure in the Pentecostal faith. He is, in fact, "...the author and finisher of our faith" (Heb. 12:2a). In the Pentecostal mind, the name of Jesus connotes the same Deity as the names by which Yahweh is known. Jesus is Savior, Shepherd, Almighty God, Baptizer in the Holy Spirit, Healer and Physician, Prince of Peace, Provider, Redeemer, and returning King. A primary goal of Pentecostals, then, is to gain and maintain intimate fellowship with God through Christ.

The apostle Paul, in his epistle to the Philippian Church, compares the value of his relationship with Christ and his own pedigree and reputation. He says,

> *But what things were gain to me, those I counted loss for Christ. Yea doubtless, and I count all things but loss for the excellency of the knowledge of Christ Jesus my Lord: for whom I have suffered the loss of all things, and do count them but dung, that I may win Christ* (Philippians 3:7-8).

In other words, Paul, who referred to himself as "a Hebrew of the Hebrews" (Phil. 3:5), considered it an even greater honor that he was a Christian. But Paul did not stop there. For he went on to state that his heart's desire was, "That I may know Him [Christ], and the power of His resurrection, and the fellowship of His sufferings, being made conformable unto His death" (Phil. 3:10).

Paul wanted to be associated with the entirety of Christ's experience, including both the joys and the sorrows. The Greek word for *know* in this passage is *Ginosko*, which connotes having an intimate relationship with another. This word corresponds closely with the Hebrew word, *Yada*, that is used in Psalm 103:7, in which it is stated that God *made His ways known to Moses.*

Something within the human heart longs for a closeness with God that can only be attained through intimate fellowship. God has been revealed in human form in Jesus Christ. He is the head of the Church, which is His Body and we, through our belief and trust in Him, become partakers of His very nature. In order to know Christ well, we, too, must experience the power of His resurrection and the fellowship of His sufferings. But as Paul told Timothy, "If we suffer, we shall also reign with Him..." (2 Tim. 2:12).

The process of knowing Christ takes us far beyond an intellectual awareness of Him. As we walk with Him, and as He touches our hearts with His thoughts and desires, we are changed more and more into His image. Our own motives become influenced toward an increasing desire to do His will. For that reason,

> "Neither the high-church congregational chanting of the Apostles' Creed, nor any of the other creeds—the Nicene Creed (A.D. 325), the Niceno-Constantinopolitan Creed (A.D. 381), the Calcedonian Formula (A.D. 451), the so-called Athanasian Creed (c. A.D. 475-500), but the present experience of...Jesus...provides that transforming intimate knowledge of the Lord" (Burgess, McGee, and Alexander 1988, 481).

In closing this chapter, I should like to introduce a man who I believe has the spirit of both Moses and Paul. Although some may say that he has not achieved what we would term greatness as measured by our standards, he is doubtless, like Moses, a friend of God.

A Modern Friend of God

The Reverend Ernest L. Hardy is "Pastor Emeritus" at the Church of Christ, Apostolic Faith, in Columbus, Ohio. He is also my former pastor, and over the past several years, he and I have developed a warm and enduring friendship.

After serving as full-time pastor of the above-named assembly for 20 years, Reverend Hardy suffered two strokes in 1989 and 1991, respectively. As a result, he was left partially paralyzed and confined to a wheelchair. If I were looking for someone who might have reason to question God, it would be him. But with a body that is broken and legs that no longer carry him where he wants to go, Pastor Hardy is resolute about his faith in God.

Throughout the past two years, I have had the opportunity to visit with Pastor Hardy each week in his home. During that time, I have been the beneficiary of his unwavering witness to the love of God. In listening, I have come to realize that I am more crippled than he. For, although his natural body is restricted to that wheelchair, his spirit moves about freely in the throne room of God. And contrary to his physical appearance, he is a living testimony to God's sustaining power.

Several months ago, a certain minister came to town and spoke at Pastor Hardy's church. The minister reportedly delivered a powerful sermon, and many people were drawn by the Holy Spirit, receiving salvation and Spirit baptism. In an atmosphere that was charged with excitement and anticipation, the minister walked over to Pastor Hardy and began to talk with him about being healed from his physical paralysis. After praying for him, the minister requested that several men lift Pastor Hardy from his wheelchair. As they stood him on his feet, the minister asked Pastor Hardy to walk across the floor. He made several attempts but was unsuccessful. As Pastor Hardy was placed back into his wheelchair, and in the presence of several hundred observers, the minister leaned over to Pastor Hardy and suggested to him that he must continue to believe God for his healing, thus inferring that at that time he lacked the faith required to secure his miracle.

For many weeks afterward, Pastor Hardy and I discussed this event. He was deeply concerned about whether he had in some way demonstrated a lack of faith. As we continued to discuss and pray about it, he gained more confidence in the fact that as much as he genuinely wanted to be healed, both then and now, there was nothing lacking in his relationship with God—including too little faith— that caused him to forfeit his miracle. Had Pastor Hardy's fellowship with God not been secure, this most recent experience would have left him devastated.

Although I am not blaming anyone for what happened to Pastor Hardy, I have gained a deeper insight regarding the business of

Heaven. I have also discovered a powerful principle in the Kingdom of God: *Without the anointing of God, the rod is just a stick; and without the direction of God, the rod brings Him no glory.*

As we attempt to minister to the needs of hurting people, wherever they may be and whatever their condition, we must remain sensitive to the leading of the Holy Spirit. In our efforts to impart the life of God to others, we must avoid—even disdain—the temptation to take God's matters into our own hands, no matter how powerful our passions may be to the contrary. After all, someone else's life is at stake.

Is Pastor Hardy pleased that he is in this condition? No, he is not. Would he rather be healed and whole again? Yes, without a doubt. Like all of us, Pastor Hardy would prefer that life be more convenient. At times, he has become wearied and has wondered why he has had to carry such a heavy burden. But he has not given up on God. This modern-day Moses has escaped the psychological enslavement of his physical condition. He has crossed the "Red Sea" of despair and has entered into the "Promised Land" of intimate fellowship with God.

It would be easy for Pastor Hardy to sit on the sidelines, letting others carry forward the torch of faith. And although this wounded warrior no longer ministers publicly, he remains an enthusiastic voice for God, publishing a weekly article in the church bulletin. Without the full use of his hands, Pastor Hardy records his material on cassette tape and his daughter, Marsha, transcribes it for publication. Central to this spiritual warrior's ministry is the testimony of the prophet Habakkuk who said:

> *Although the fig tree shall not blossom, neither shall fruit be in the vines; the labour of the olive shall fail, and the fields shall yield no meat; the flock shall be cut off from the fold, and there shall be no herd in the stalls: yet I will rejoice in the Lord, I will joy in the God of my salvation* (Habakkuk 3:17-18).

At first glance, this reads like a confession of fatalistic resignation. It is, instead, a proclamation of one's absolute confidence in his/her fellowship with God.

Pastor Hardy continues to rejoice in the fact that he is a son of God, and his prayers are not those of complaint, but of thanksgiving. He is convinced that God's glory is perfected in us as we learn to worship Him in this manner. "Thank you, my friend, for teaching me this profound truth."

Conclusion

Genuine fellowship with God is not developed via a prepackaged formula or by memorizing a few Bible verses. God does not reside in theological creeds or in denominational doctrines. He lives in and He works primarily through people. We must let God be God in our lives. Solomon said, "Trust in the Lord with all thine heart; and lean not unto thine own understanding. In all thy ways acknowledge Him and He shall direct thy paths" (Prov. 3:5-6).

I believe that God desires to find people who want to know Him and who want Him to occupy the throne of leadership in their lives. He wants to lead and guide us in all aspects of our lives. His hopes and dreams concerning us are designed to be fulfilled in large measure through us. He has established the means whereby we may enter into covenant with Him and benefit from His ongoing fellowship. Let us set aside time on our agenda to know God!

Challenge Questions

1. In the light of biblical evidence, why is there such a divergence of opinion regarding God's true identity?
2. Why must intimacy with God be a function of our worship and not just come as the result of our study?
3. Why is it impossible for us as Pentecostals to separate the practice of our faith from an understanding of the life of God?
4. In what ways might the Pentecostal community witness the glory of God that was revealed unto Moses?
5. How might the strategy of knowing God intimately become a standard for all believers?

References

Arthur, Kay. *To Know Him by Name*. Sisters, OR: Multromah Books, 1995.

Burgess, Stanley M., Gary B. McGee, and Patrick H. Alexander, eds. *Dictionary of Pentecostal and Charismatic Movements*. Grand Rapids, MI: Zondervan Publishing House, 1988.

Horton, Stanley M., ed. *Systematic Theology: A Pentecostal Perspective*. Springfield, MO: Logion Press, 1994.

Horton, Stanley M., and William W. Menzies. *Bible Doctrines: A pentecostal Perspective*. Springfield, MO: Gospel Publishing House, 1994.

Chapter 10

Live Within the Will of God

And he [Abraham] *believed in the Lord; and He counted it to him for righteousness* (Genesis 15:6).

We were challenged in the previous chapter to know God. A second challenge, and one that is inextricably linked with the first, is to know our rights as covenant partners with God and then to live in fulfillment of those rights. As we seek to achieve that goal, we need a standard or rule by which God may be understood. The most notable standard is His Word. Therein are we given a progressive and revelatory picture of His nature, character, acts, and will. In the present chapter, we shall first focus our attention upon the concept of "will" and how it may be applied to a discussion of our relationship with Almighty God. Next, we will address the concept of "will" as it is presented in the Bible, the book that contains God's story of redemption. Finally, we shall review the provisions of the Old and New Blood Covenants and discuss their importance to all believers.

Will: Three Connotations

In common usage, the term *will*, may be described as: (1) an attitude, (2) an ability, and (3) an assignment. As an attitude, *will* may be described as the predisposition or forethought that occurs prior to a given act. It might also be called *motive*. Almighty God created us and gave us the right to make choices. We remain His property, yet we possess the legal authority to act from our own free choice.

Human will is a powerful force, not only involving forethought and choice, but also giving psychological fuel to most of our actions. Championship athletes often speak of "willing" themselves to extraordinary performances. Moreover, it is common to hear stories of earthquake victims who, although buried beneath the rubble of fallen buildings, have lived for days on the strength of their will to survive.

Although the term *will* involves an attitude that precedes behavior, a second aspect involves the ability to perform something that one desires. For instance, *will* is the relative power exerted by one competitor against another in a contest. A group of 300-pound defensive linemen in the NFL exerts tremendous force and will as they seek to overcome their offensive counterparts en route to a quarterback sack.

It should be noted at this point that the desire to succeed is insufficient without the accompanying ability to get the job done. I am less than six feet tall, and I cannot will myself to improve upon that. I am limited by certain genetic constraints that cannot be overcome.

A third connotation of *will* is that of an assignment of inheritance. One subject, usually an individual, bequeaths to others some portion of his/her assets upon the occasion of his/her death. The bequeathing subject, known as a *testator*, draws up a *Last Will And Testament*. This document is a type of covenant. As a binding agreement between the testator and his/her heirs, a will contains a listing of items within the testator's estate and specifies which of those items each heir is to receive. In order for a will to be enacted, it must bear the testator's signature. Although there are some exceptions, as a rule this signing is witnessed by a Notary Public, a licensed government agent, who affixes an official seal to the will. The purpose of the witness is to verify the identity of the testator and to attest to the fact that he/she is mentally capable to act in a responsible manner. Once signed and notarized, the will is registered in the appropriate local court and becomes an official public document. The will is enforced upon the testator's death.

In summary, then, the term *will* may be used to describe the motive or forethought behind certain actions, the ability to perform those actions, and the assignment of inheritance rights and privileges by one party to others. We shall use this three-pronged paradigm in our study of the will of God.

The Will of God

The *will of God* includes His attitude, His ability, and His assignment of inheritance. The attitude of God about Himself and His position is clear: "I am the first, and I am the last; and beside Me there is no God" (Is. 44:6b). Further, He offers, "...I am the Lord; and there is none else" (Is. 45:18). As God, He has no rival or competitor. Isaiah said, "All nations before Him are as nothing; and they are counted to Him less than nothing, and vanity" (Is. 40:17). God acts out of His own predisposition. David said, "The counsel of the Lord standeth for ever, the thoughts of His heart to all generations" (Ps. 33:11). In Genesis 1:3-25, God's creative work in nature sprang forth as He gave the verbal commands to "Let there be...and it was so." From the depths of His own divine counsel, He said, "...Let us make man in Our image, after Our likeness..." (Gen. 1:26). Moses tells us, "So God created man in His own image, in the image of God created He him; male and female created He them" (Gen. 1:27).

God's will also includes His ability. The statement, "Let us make man...," was based on God's power to perform His desires. Isaiah said, "It is He that sitteth upon the circle of the earth, and the inhabitants thereof are as grasshoppers; that stretcheth out the heavens as a curtain, and spreadeth them out as a tent to dwell in" (Is. 40:22). We have previously observed that among the constitutional attributes of God, He is all-powerful, all-knowing, and He fills all space. Therefore, He is limitless in all respects. John said of Him, "All things were made by Him; and without Him was not any thing made that was made" (Jn. 1:3). God is able!

God's will is not limited to what He wants to do or is capable of doing, but it includes all that He has promised to leave for us who believe Him. Yahweh, the I AM, is a covenant-keeping God, having promised to redeem all people who seek His fellowship. He knew that sin-filled creatures like us would never be able to attain His level of holiness without His help. Not only that, but we also have nothing to offer in return for His kindness. With a heart of love and a hand of compassion, God has made provision for our eternal future. Much of what we may learn of His purpose and plan in this regard is presented in the Bible, the written Word of God.

The Bible: An Overview

The Bible is a sacred document that contains God's purpose and plan of redemption. It is a complete volume, inspired and authored by the Holy Spirit. Forty different individuals, from Moses to John the Revelator, were commissioned, inspired, and empowered by the Holy Spirit to inscribe God's Word. Writing in unity, though not together, these ordinary men included, "princes, kings, priests, prophets, herdsmen, farm laborers, fishermen, tax collectors, physicians, lawyers, and teachers" (Purkizer 1955, 44). Although some had the use of other scriptural portions as they wrote, none had access to all the other books at one time. And no writer was aware that his work would become part of "the Bible."

Structural Outline

The Bible is one book of many books. The Hebrew Bible, written over a thousand-year period (1500-400 B.C.), contains 24 books organized into three sections: the Law (Torah), the Prophets (former and latter), and the Writings (poetical books, five scrolls, historical books).

The Protestant version of the Bible contains 66 separate books and is divided into two main sections: the Old Testament and the New Testament. The Old Testament is organized into 39 books, 15 more than the Hebrew Bible, but having the same content. The Old Testament contains four main divisions: the Law (Penteteuch), history, poetry, and prophecy. The New Testament, consisting of 27 books, was written during the period A.D. 45-95 (Gromacki 1974, 48).

It is also divided into four sections: the Gospels, Acts, the Epistles (general and Pauline), and the Apocalypse (Revelation). The Roman Catholic Bible contains 11 additional books that are not included in the Protestant Canon. Known collectively as the Apocrypha, these appear to have been written between 200 B.C. and A.D. 100 (Gromacki 1974, 56).

The original languages of the Old Testament were Hebrew and Aramaic, and the New Testament was written in Greek. The interplay between the two sections of the Bible forms an indivisible whole. Purkizer says, "There are more than 250 direct quotations from the Old Testament to be found in the New" (Purkizer 1995, 48). The Church has long held to the position that the Scriptures are unified:

"The New is in the Old contained,
The Old is in the New explained:
The New is in the Old concealed,
The Old is in the New Revealed" (Gromacki 1974, 42-43).

The connection between the Old and New Testaments is not incidental. Purkizer offers that "...One scholar lists a total of 1,603 quotations, references, and allusions which link the New Testament with the Old" (Purkizer 1955, 48). Jesus based all His scriptural teaching upon material within the Hebrew Bible (the Old Testament). The chart below demonstrates the structural parallelism that exists between the organization of the Old and New Testaments in the Protestant Bible (also Fig. 10.1).

Parallelism of the Old and New Testaments (Purkizer 1955, 46)

		Old Testament	New Testament
A.	History	The Penteteuch The Historical Books	The Gospels The Acts
B.	Interpretation and Application	The Poetical and Wisdom Books	The Pauline Epistles The General Epistles
C.	Prophecy	The Major Prophets The Minor Prophets	Revelation

(Fig. 10.1)   **OLD AND NEW TESTAMENT PARALLELS OF GOD'S WORD**

Although the Bible is a clear story of God's redemptive purpose, it is not written as a novel with a simplistic plot. The Bible sometimes appears to be in disagreement with itself. Some biblical events offer no obvious explanation regarding God's motive or direction. "If, however, the Bible is viewed as a drama, one allows for the element of progression and newness, while at the same time affirming the unity of the Scriptures" (Ewart 1983, 26). As we approach God's Word with an attitude of reverent expectation, we can be certain that we will not come away empty.

The Bible Contains Legal Provisions

The Bible is not just a story about God. It contains God's *Covenant of Promise.* Within its pages, God has outlined the resources in His estate and has established a mechanism whereby individuals may become His heirs. The agreement carries the signature of God, has been executed by a blood sacrifice, and carries the seal of witness as prescribed by law.

The Hebrew word for "covenant" is *Berith,* and the Greek word is *Diatheke.* In further clarifying the fundamental meaning of a covenant, one writer says that "...it is an agreement to 'cut a covenant by the shedding of blood and walking between pieces of flesh' " (Booker 1981, 26-27). Implicit in the idea of a covenant is the exchanging of rights and responsibilities by the agreeing parties. Such things as property sharing, rights of inheritance, and aid in fighting one's enemies are included in the provisions of a covenant. In the biblical context, blessings and cursings accompany obedience or disobedience to such an agreement.

The Bible Is God's Word

No one has ever seen the Spirit of God (see Jn. 1:18). How, then, can we confidently trust and believe Him? How can we know that He will make good on His promises toward us? Balaam, soothsayer of the Midianites, even though pressured to say otherwise, had to confess, "God is not a man, that He should lie; neither the son of man, that He should repent: hath He said, and shall He not do it? or hath He spoken, and shall He not make it good?" (Num. 23:19)

The Bible is a message from the heart of God. He guarantees it, stands behind it, and makes it sure.

God could find no greater than Himself and has, therefore, sworn by Himself that His Word is true. The Bible testifies to the following (also Fig. 10.2):

- God's Word is co-existent and co-equal with Him: John said, "In the beginning was the Word, and the Word was with God, and the Word was God. The same was in the beginning with God" (Jn. 1:1-2);
- God's Word is immutable. It cannot be changed or refuted: The prophet Isaiah heard God saying, "So shall My word be that goeth forth out of My mouth: it shall not return unto Me void, but it shall accomplish that which I please, and it shall prosper in the thing whereto I sent it" (Is. 55:11);
- God's Word is creational: The writer of the Book of Hebrews said, "Through faith we understand that the worlds were framed by the word of God, so that things which are seen were not made of things which do appear" (Heb. 11:3). The apostle Paul offered that God, "...calleth those things which be not as though they were" (Rom. 4:17);
- God's Word is manifested in a person: Again, John the apostle says, "And the Word was made flesh, and dwelt among us, (and we beheld His glory, the glory as of the only begotten of the Father,) full of grace and truth" (Jn. 1:14);
- God's Word is life: John says, "In Him [the Word] was life; and the life was the light of men" (Jn. 1:4). John further states, "...this is the record, that God hath given to us eternal life, and this life is in His Son" (1 Jn. 5:11). In the context of His claim to be the Son of God, Jesus stated boldly, "...the words that I speak unto you, they are spirit, and they are life" (Jn. 6:63);
- God's Word is eternal: Jesus said, "Heaven and earth shall pass away, but My words shall not pass away" (Mt. 24:35);
- Jesus is God's living Word: The author of the Book of the Revelation tells us what he saw in his vision of the last

things. Referring to Jesus, the apostle John said, "And I saw heaven opened, and behold a white horse; and he that sat upon him was called Faithful and True.... And He was clothed with a vesture dipped in blood: and His name is called The Word of God" (Rev. 19:11-13).

(Fig. 10.2) **THE NATURE OF GOD'S WORD**

We have seen that the Bible is essentially a dramatic and progressive revelation of God. In addition, it is an expression of God's will: His attitude, His ability, and the assignment of His inheritance.

Most importantly, the Bible contains God's *Eternal Will and Testament*. It is a binding agreement—a Covenant of Blood.

A Covenant of Blood

The concept of a blood covenant is both historical and sacred. E.W. Kenyon states that, "The Blood Covenant, or what we call the Lord's Table, is based upon the oldest known covenant in the human family...It is evident that God cut or entered into a covenant with Adam at the very beginning" (Kenyon 1969, 7). God has always wanted to be in fellowship with us.

Not only is the blood covenant historically significant, but it is sacred as well. A blood covenant represents the deepest level of mutual commitment between two parties. Kenyon offers that it is, "...a perpetual covenant, indissoluble, a covenant that cannot be annulled" (Kenyon 1969, 10). The Bible contains two distinctive covenants of God: the Old Blood Covenant and the New Blood Covenant. Although I must admit that throughout my entire Christian experience I have not understood this concept, I have come to realize that appropriating the provisions of God's Blood Covenant spells the difference between life and death for the believer.

The Old Covenant

God initiated the Old Covenant with Abraham. In this agreement, God called Abram, as he was then known, from Ur of the Chaldees and brought him to the land of Canaan. He promised this land to Abram and to his descendants as an inheritance. God also promised Abram that he would be the progenitor of an eternal seed (Israel), the number of which would be *as the dust of the earth, the stars of heaven, and the sand on the seashore* (see Gen. 12:1-3; 13:16; 22:17).

God was so committed to His promise that He swore an oath to Himself that He would keep His word (Gen. 22:16; Heb. 6:13-14; Ps. 105:9; Lk. 1:73). In the context of that oath, God entered into covenant with Abram. The ceremony in which God "cut covenant" with Abram is recorded in Genesis chapter 15.

God instructed Abram: "...Take me an heifer of three years old, and a she goat of three years old, and a ram of three years old, and a turtledove, and a young pigeon" (Gen. 15:9). Abram then killed the heifer, the goat, and the ram, and split them down the middle, laying the pieces side by side. This procedure was an indication that both God and Abram had a substitute sacrifice at the ceremony. The shedding of the animals' blood was the "signing" phase of the covenant process.

God then put Abram to sleep, thus bypassing his flesh (his intellectual reasoning), and spoke into his spirit the provisions of the divine promise. He told Abram that his seed, those of the nation of Israel, would be servants in a strange land for a period of 400 years. God added, "...and afterward shall they come out with great substance" (Gen. 15:14). God also promised Abram a long and peaceful life. As he was awakened, Abram saw what appeared to be "...a smoking furnace, and a burning lamp..." (Gen. 15:17), passing between the pieces of the sacrifice. Richard Booker describes the smoking furnace and the burning lamp:

> "Abram sees Christ walking in his place. Christ, the eternal Son of God, in his pre-existing glory, cut covenant with God the Father and stood in for Abram. He is the only one who could stand in for Abram. And all of Abram's seed were included in the covenant because they were in Abram" (Booker 1981, 47-48).

The imagery and truth that stands out in this description is a powerful testimony, not only to the oneness of God, but to the extent of His commitment to His new covenant partner. Abram, a sinner who was incapable of entering into a covenant with Almighty God, now had an Intermediary who could represent him fully and completely before the Father.

God later changed Abram's name to *Abraham* and promised that the covenant that they had just entered into would last forever: "And I will establish My covenant between Me and thee and thy seed after thee in their generations for an everlasting covenant, to be a God unto thee, and to thy seed after thee" (Gen. 17:7).

The Seal of Witness

The second phase in instituting the Old Covenant involved the legalization of the Covenant with a *seal*. It was mentioned in our earlier description of a Last Will and Testament that the seal is a certifying witness to the integrity of the testator.

Under the Old Blood Covenant, God placed His seal or "mark" on Abraham's flesh through the rite of circumcision (see Gen. 17:10-14). God instructed Abraham to perform this ritual on all male babies on the eighth day after birth, and on all Jewish converts. Accordingly, circumcision has been regarded as, "...the supreme obligatory sign of loyalty and adherence to Judaism" (Werblowsky and Wigoder 1965, 90). Because of the Old Blood Covenant, Abraham and his descendants could count on Almighty God as the source for all their needs throughout eternity. The redemptive names of God listed in Chapter 9 of the present text (i.e. Healer, Peace, Shield, Righteousness, etc.) are indicative of the benefits that He shares with His covenant partners.

The Principle of Exclusive Inclusivity

The Old Blood Covenant was exclusive in the respect that it focused upon Abraham's seed as the chosen heirs of God's promise. Four hundred years after the initiation of this agreement, God delivered Israel from Egyptian slavery. At that time, He reiterated His promise to them with a clear condition: "Now therefore, if ye will obey My voice indeed, and keep My covenant, then ye shall be a peculiar treasure unto Me above all people: for all the earth is Mine" (Ex. 19:5). God later reminded them that they were a "...holy people unto the Lord thy God: the Lord thy God hath chosen thee to be a special people unto Himself, above all people that are upon the face of the earth" (Deut. 7:6). Israel's covenant benefits would be predicated upon their obedience to God's Law.

But the Old Covenant was inclusive as well. The particularity of Israel's choosing was in the context of God's promise to Abraham that his seed would be a source of blessing to the entire world: "...in thee [in your seed] shall all the families of the earth be blessed"

(Gen. 12:3). The Old Blood Covenant legally preserved the integrity of the Abrahamic line, thus clearing the way for the birth of Jesus Christ. It was He who established the means whereby all people, both Jew and non-Jew, could be reconciled into fellowship with God. This brings us to the second of God's major promises—the New Blood Covenant.

The New Blood Covenant

It may be accurately said that the Old Testament is, in fact, a first installment toward God's final and ultimate reconciliation of mankind. The fulfillment of the promise is found in the second part of God's will, the New Blood Covenant. This section of the will is both historical and prophetic. The New Covenant is historical in that it is built upon principles established under the Old Covenant. The process of swearing an oath and shedding blood from a pure sacrifice was the continuation of a principle that God had established under the old order.

The prophetic nature of the New Covenant is evident in the fact that, even as it looks back to the Old Covenant for its foundation, it begins with Christ and looks forward into the future. The New joins in perfect harmony with the Old in proclaiming the time when "...The kingdoms of this world are become the kingdoms of our Lord, and of His Christ; and He shall reign for ever and ever" (Rev. 11:15). Daniel said of Christ, "And there was given Him dominion, and glory, and a kingdom, that all people, nations, and languages, should serve Him: His dominion is an everlasting dominion, which shall not pass away, and His kingdom that which shall not be destroyed" (Dan. 7:14).

Paul said that Christ willingly "...humbled Himself, and became obedient unto death, even the death of the cross" (Phil. 2:8). He became, therefore, the *Testator* of the New Blood Covenant (see Heb. 9:15-18). He was also the sin-sacrifice, the Lamb slain before the foundation of the world (see Rev. 13:8). The sinless blood of Christ was shed so that all who were lost and would believe on Him might be redeemed unto God (see Rev. 5:9-12; 22:1). The writer to the Hebrews said of this sacrificial offering,

For where a testament is, there must also of necessity be the death of the testator. For a testament is of force after men are dead: otherwise it is of no strength at all while the testator liveth. ... So Christ was once offered to bear the sins of many; and unto them that look for Him shall He appear the second time without sin unto salvation (Hebrews 9:16-17, 28).

Jesus Christ removed the genetic and legal constraints that prevented all non-Jews from coming into the rights and privileges of God's Covenants. The death, burial, resurrection, and ascension of Christ represents the cornerstone of the Christian faith. As a result of His complete obedience to the Father, Jesus prayed, "I have glorified Thee on the earth: I have finished the work which Thou gavest Me to do" (Jn. 17:4). Later, while hanging on Golgotha's cross, He said again, with no pretension, "...It is finished..." (Jn. 19:30). In other words, payment of the sin debt was made once and for all.

Jesus has become the "knot" in the center, tying together two separate pieces of rope. He alone resolves the conflict between the original Jewish heirs to the Old Blood Covenant and those who have been adopted and grafted into God's family through the New Blood Covenant.

Heirs to the Will: Israel

For the Jew, the Covenant of God is unalterable and eternal. God said,

But this shall be the covenant that I will make with the house of Israel; After those days, saith the Lord, I will put My law in their inward parts, and write it in their hearts; and will be their God, and they shall be My people (Jeremiah 31:33).

Within the Christian community, and particularly among Pentecostals, there is a theological preference to interpret this text as an exclusive reference to the New Testament Church. This thesis promotes the idea that God has bypassed the Jewish nation in favor of the non-Jewish *Spiritual Israel*. The apostle Paul, himself a converted Pharisee, considered the question of whether or not God had rejected His people, Israel. With much conviction, Paul answered with a resounding, "God forbid. For I also am an Israelite, of the seed of Abraham, of the tribe of Benjamin" (Rom. 11:1). Paul's position was that Israel's initial disobedience and God's subsequent judgment of her made room in God's redemptive plan for the Gentile race.

> *...Have they stumbled that they should fall? God forbid: but rather through their fall salvation is come unto the Gentiles, for to provoke them to jealousy. Now if the fall of them be the riches of the world, and the diminishing of them the riches of the Gentiles; how much more their fulness?* (Romans 11:11)

Menzies and Horton echo Paul's sentiments, saying, "Surely this makes it clear that God has not thrown aside His people!" (Menzies and Horton 1994, 236). Popular Christian thought to the contrary, the Bible is consistent in rehearsing God's promise that Israel has not been forsaken.

Hocken has summarized Israel's current place in the heart of God:

> "For Paul, then, the promises of God to Israel endure. The original promise of restoration following repentance still stands (Rom. 11:23). They remain 'chosen'; they remain Israelites to whom belong the sonship, the glory, the covenants, the giving of the law, the worship, and the promises; to them belong the patriarchs, and of their race, according to the flesh is the Christ.... Israel's place in God's plan is not cancelled" (Hocken 1994, 135).

The covenant between God and His chosen people, Israel, is immutable and, therefore, cannot be nullified. The challenge to Israel, however, as well as to all nations, is to believe in the finished work of Christ and to confess that "Jesus Christ is Lord, to the glory of God the Father" (Phil. 2:11b). Although we have not yet seen the complete fulfillment of this challenge, the Word of God offers that this, in fact, will be part of Israel's future.

Again, we should note that, "Ezekiel 36:24-27 shows God will bring Israel out of all countries and will bring them back to their own land. Then He will cleanse them, restore them spiritually, and put His Spirit within them" (Menzies and Horton 1994, 237). God's witness to the world through His chosen people will be performed! But praise be to God, His arms of salvation are opened wide enough to receive all others who will believe in His Word.

Heirs to the Will: The Church

Under the Old Covenant, God signed the agreement with the sacrificial blood of a pure animal, and He sealed it through the rite of circumcision. In order for the New Covenant to be valid, it had to satisfy the same essential requirements as the Old. God, therefore, had to provide a blood sacrifice as a ransom for sin, and a type of circumcision had to occur in the hearts of men and women that we might bear the seal as God's redeemed.

In the New Blood Covenant, we are introduced to the idea of spiritual circumcision. God has given the Holy Spirit as the "Seal" or Official Witness to the fact of our right to God's inheritance through Christ. Paul testified that:

The Spirit itself beareth witness with our spirit, that we are the children of God: and if children, then heirs; heirs of God, and joint-heirs with Christ; if so be that we suffer with Him, that we may be also glorified together (Romans 8:16-17).

And to the Colossian Church, he said:

And ye are complete in Him [that is, in Christ], *which is the head of all principality and power: in whom also ye are circumcised with the circumcision made without hands, in putting off the body of the sins of the flesh by the circumcision of Christ* (Colossians 2:10-11).

Christ is Messiah, *the Anointed One of God.* As a result of His death, both for us and instead of us, we are no longer expected to gain right standing with God through legalistic or genetic means alone. Paul said to the Church at Rome:

For he is not a Jew, which is one outwardly; neither is that circumcision, which is outward in the flesh: but he is a Jew, which is one inwardly; and circumcision is that of the heart, in the spirit, and not in the letter; whose praise is not of men, but of God (Romans 2:28-29).

For the Gentile world, the promise from God is just as sure: "Even as Abraham believed God, and it was accounted to him for righteousness. Know ye therefore that they which are of faith, the same are the children of Abraham" (Gal. 3:6-7). The New Covenant means a new spiritual birth. We have all sinned and come short of God's glory (see Rom. 3:23). As we confess our unrighteousness before God, and as we repent and accept His forgiveness, we receive this promise: "That if thou shalt confess with thy mouth the Lord Jesus, and shalt believe in thine heart that God hath raised Him from the dead, thou shalt be saved" (Rom. 10:9).

Paul, speaking on the effect of our new birth in Christ, admonished us that, "...if any man be in Christ, he is a new creature: old things are passed away; behold, all things are become new" (2 Cor. 5:17). As we receive the life of God through Christ, we become "fellowcitizens with the saints, and of the household of God" (Eph. 2:19b). We are the righteousness of God in Christ, entitled to the benefits of God's covenant. "For in Christ Jesus neither circumcision availeth any thing, nor uncircumcision, but a new creature" (Gal. 6:15).

In the Book of Revelation, John heard Jesus say, "I am Alpha and Omega, the beginning and the ending, saith the Lord, which is, and which was, and which is to come..." (Rev. 1:8). Jesus stands firmly planted on an ageless line of eternal truth, encompassing all time—past, present, and future. In order to retain the authenticity of Christianity in general, and of Pentecostalism in particular, we must recognize the historicity of God's progressive work among mankind. We must keep sacred the memory of the foundation that God has established in the Old Blood Covenant.

It is inaccurate to begin a teaching of God's redemptive plan with a discussion of the baby Jesus lying in Bethlehem's manger. A strictly Gentile perspective such as this is myopic (shortsighted) in that it ignores the roots of that plan in the Old Covenant. As such, it has no validity in the Kingdom of God. Equally inaccurate is the conclusion within Orthodox Jewry that *Torah* (the Law of Moses) represents the totality of God's revelation and that Judaism is a closed system.

The Word of God is full of promise, and He is continuously seeking those who would embrace Him and by faith, join His family. To Jew and Gentile alike, Christ has become, "…our peace, who hath made both one, and hath broken down the middle wall of partition between us. … For through Him we both have access by one Spirit unto the Father" (Eph. 2:14,18). God has demonstrated His love in offering Christ as our Redeemer. As all have been concluded under the Law, so may all be included in God by faith in Jesus Christ. "And if ye be Christ's, then are ye Abraham's seed, and heirs according to the promise" (Gal. 3:29).

Synthesizing and Conforming to God's Will

It is God's will that:

- We know Him and that we have intimate fellowship with Him;
- We live above the curse of the law of sin and death;
- We exercise dominion and stewardship over His creation;
- We live in peace with Him and with all humankind;
- We experience a healthy lifestyle—spiritually, physically, emotionally, and intellectually;
- We live in obedience to His Word;
- We abide in and become like Christ;
- We bear the fruit of the Holy Spirit;
- We have the eternal life of God forever;
- His glory be revealed within us upon the earth, the same as it is in Heaven.

The challenge for us is to discover how to conform to this God-designed purpose and to live in accordance with our discovery each day. God spoke these words through Solomon:

My son, attend to My words; incline thine ear unto My sayings. Let them not depart from thine eyes; keep them in the midst of thine heart. For they are life unto those that find them, and health to all their flesh (Proverbs 4:20-22).

Conformity to God's Word is synonymous with conformity to His will.

Foundations of a Bible-Based Lifestyle

The objectives of this chapter would not be fulfilled without addressing the practical question of how we might learn to live a Bible-based lifestyle. I should like to outline several basic but important steps toward accomplishing this requirement.

First of all, *we should own a Bible.* The Protestant Bible, which was referred to earlier in this chapter, includes the entire 66 books of the Old and New Testaments. Today, there are numerous translations of the modern Bible in print, so that making a selection of the best one is a matter of personal choice.

Second, since much of the biblical text is challenging to read and to understand, we should also *own a Bible summary and a Bible commentary.* Christian bookstores carry a wide selection of such teaching material that can be extremely helpful in navigating the Scriptures.

Owning the most expensive Bible and all the best explanatory material, however, cannot substitute for being exposed to an environment of anointed Bible teaching. This leads us to the third and perhaps the most difficult step in the process. *We need to be actively involved in a thriving fellowship of Christian believers, a place in which the full gospel message is being taught and practiced.* Because of the sheer number of churches that are "open for business," this critical step must be taken prayerfully and under the guidance of the Holy Spirit.

Great care must be exercised in selecting that place where we entrust others to assist in the development of our relationship with God. In this regard, the following checklist of questions might be helpful in evaluating a potential place of worship:

1. Are the teachings of this fellowship Bible-centered?
   a. Does the ministry actively promote the full gospel message of the life, ministry, and completed redemptive work of Jesus Christ?
   b. Does the fellowship stress the in-filling of the Holy Spirit and the operation of the Spirit's gifts within the Body of Christ?
   c. Is the doctrine of the fellowship consistent with the standards of the Christian tradition?
   d. Does the fellowship emphasize the inerrancy of God's Word?
2. Is the ministry family-oriented?
   a. Does the fellowship promote the integrity and development of family values?
   b. Are activities designed to benefit men, women, and children?
3. Are the goals and objectives of the fellowship clearly stated and available for review?
4. Is the fellowship actively involved in witnessing outside its own walls?
   a. Are there activities that focus upon the larger community?
   b. Are there activities that focus directly or indirectly upon ministry to foreign lands?
5. Do opportunities exist for discovering, developing, and practicing one's God-given talents?

We are not just believers; we are consumers as well. Although the above list may seem objective and business-oriented, it must be noted that our fellowship with God is worthy of serious consideration. These criteria should be used, not as an absolute measuring rod, but as a helpful tool in determining how we might find the best possible environment for our spiritual growth.

The fourth step in building a Bible-centered lifestyle is *to practice a regular daily schedule of personal worship and prayer.* Whether it is for five minutes or for an hour, this activity promotes a sense of inner peace and keeps us in alignment with the thoughts of God.

The Bible, God's Word and Covenant, is to be a continuous lamp unto our feet and a light unto our path (see Ps. 119:105). God uses His Word to draw us to Him. We, then, are responsible for nurturing our fellowship with Him.

A Word of Warning

Humanized religious thought has polluted some against the clear message of God's redemptive promise. The number who claim to be *God's chosen few* is so large that it has become inestimable. Conversely, those who really believe God and take Him at His Word are difficult to identify.

If we fail to see the finished work of Christ as God's grace given to all who are lost, then we will demean the efficacy of His Word in us. John, writing on the Isle of Patmos, ended his famous Apocalypse with a stern warning for those who would add to or detract from the inerrant Word of God:

> *For I testify unto every man that heareth the words of the prophecy of this book, If any man shall add unto these things, God shall add unto him the plagues that are written in this book: and if any man shall take away from the words of the book of this prophecy, God shall take away his part out of the book of life, and out of the holy city, and from the things which are written in this book* (Revelation 22:18-19).

Conclusion

The Bible presents a progressive outline of God's unfolding plan to redeem mankind. God's *Eternal Will And Testament* clearly states that those who believe and walk in His statutes will share in His inheritance. In this chapter, we have explored the lengths to which God has gone in order that we might be saved.

In the Old Blood Covenant, God exclusively selected the nation of Israel to be recipients of His love, mercy, and grace. Through His relationship with Israel, God demonstrated how He draws each of us to Him and how He works with us to achieve the goal of our perfection in Him. Through the New Blood Covenant, all who are sinners and unregenerate before God may now stand before Him righteous, in the name and authority of Jesus Christ.

When we are facing situations in our lives, when our backs are against the wall, we can find renewed strength in the pages of the "Will of God." Should we feel overwhelmed by sickness, depression, or anything, we only need to consult the Will. This is not a poetic plea for a mind over matter strategy that will leave us frustrated and disillusioned. God, who stands behind every promise He makes, offers each of us the opportunity to secure our future forever in Him. Let us choose to seek, to understand, and to walk in *God's Will.*

Challenge Questions

1. How can we, as Pentecostals, effectively distinguish between revelation and interpretation of God's Word?
2. If the Bible is to be an effective tool for understanding the heart of God, what is the responsibility of the Church and the believer in this regard?
3. In what ways does Pentecostalism reflect a "particularistic" view of God's revelation?
4. If this is a problem, what can we do to correct it?
5. What role should Pentecostals play in addressing the issue of religious bigotry and intolerance, especially in America?

References

Booker, Richard. *The Miracle of the Scarlet Thread.* Shippensburg, PA: Destiny Image Publishers, 1981.

Ewart, David. *A General Introduction to the Bible.* Grand Rapids, MI: Zondervan Publishing House, 1983.

Grumacki, Robert G. *New Testament Survey.* Grand Rapids, MI: Baker Book House, 1974.

Hocken, Peter. *The Glory and the Shame*. Guiford, Surrey: Eagle, an imprint of Inter Publishing Service, 1994.

Kenyon, E.W. *The Blood Covenant*. Lynnwood, WA: Kenyon's Gospel Publishing Society, 1969.

Menzies, William W., and Stanley M. Horton. *Bible Doctrines, A Pentecostal Perspective*. Springfield, MO: Logion Press, 1994.

Purkizer, W.T., ed. *Exploring the Old Testament*. Kansas City, MO: Beacon Hill Press, 1995.

Werblowsky, R.J., and Geoffrey Wigoder, eds. *The Encyclopedia of the Jewish Religion*. New York, Chicago, San Francisco: Holt, Rinehart, and Winston, Inc., 1965.

Chapter 11

Seek First the Kingdom of God

...Thine is the kingdom, O Lord, and Thou art exalted as head above all (1 Chronicles 29:11).

This chapter is designed to provide a workable framework within which the concept of the Kingdom of God may be examined. The goal herein is to present a third challenge for gaining fruitful fellowship with God. As with all of the material in this text, I trust that this information will be planted into our spirits, and that we will water it with the truth of God's Word and with our own faithful pursuit of His will.

Jesus said, "But seek ye first the kingdom of God, and His righteousness; and all these things [whatever you need in order to succeed in God] shall be added unto you" (Mt. 6:33). Our ultimate and overriding passion must be to please God. That goal is accomplished as we maintain fellowship with Him and as we dedicate ourselves to the performance of His will. We will promote the Kingdom of God as we continually say with our hearts, our lips, and our lives, "Thy kingdom come. Thy will be done in earth, as it is in heaven" (Mt. 6:10).

The term *Kingdom of God* is a spiritual concept. As such, it is difficult to describe in purely human terminology. Yet all spiritual ideals carry both spiritual and natural meaning and are, therefore, relevant to our daily living. God is fully aware that His glory can only be manifested through us on this earth to the extent that we carry out His will. From a common sense standpoint, that cannot

---

happen unless we are clear about how to meet His righteous standards. God is responsible for teaching us what He expects as well as for enabling us to carry it out. Note an example.

Under the Old Covenant, God issued a command to the Israelites saying, "Sanctify yourselves therefore, and be ye holy: for I am the Lord your God" (Lev. 20:7). God knew that it would be humanly impossible to meet this spiritual requirement. Without Him, it simply could not happen! Continuing, He said, "And ye shall keep my statutes, and do them: I am the Lord which sanctify you" (Lev. 20:8).

Now we get a clearer picture of how God's mandate for Israel's holiness was to be achieved: "I...sanctify you." God was saying then, as He is today, that every standard that He holds us to is only possible in the power of His might, and it is not the result of something that we do to generate His approval. As further testimony for this point, the angel of the Lord came to the prophet Zechariah saying, "...Not by might, nor by power, but by My spirit, saith the Lord of hosts" (Zech. 4:6).

All creation is under the ultimate authority and control of Almighty God. We are very much His workmanship and are, therefore, subject to Him. Our very survival demands that He stay involved with us all the time, but it also requires that we stay in close fellowship with Him—all the time. This is but one glimpse at the inner workings of the Kingdom of God. Let us look further at this spiritual concept as presented in the context of God's Word.

Scriptural Context

The term *Kingdom of God* is exclusive to the New Testament, although the principles upon which this concept is based precede the birth of Christ. The Kingdom of God is mentioned some 65 times throughout the New Testament, appearing most frequently in the Gospels (50 times). The concept is discussed primarily by Luke (30 times) and Mark (14 times). In Matthew's Gospel, we find the use of an allied term, *Kingdom of Heaven*. Although some may disagree, I believe that the terms *Kingdom of God* and *Kingdom of Heaven* are synonymous and, therefore, interchangeable. The latter term, therefore, will not be emphasized in this writing.

Jesus introduced the concept of the Kingdom of God as a natural sequel to the teachings of Judaism. In Luke's Gospel, Jesus is reported to have said, "The law and the prophets were until John: since that time the kingdom of God is preached, and every man presseth into it" (Lk. 16:16). Jesus was not implying that a new religion was being invented. Instead, He was offering that the unfolding of God's plan to redeem (buy back) lost humanity, as presented in the annals of Jewish history, was progressing to a new level.

For Jesus, the ministry of John the Baptist represented the "line of demarcation" between the Old and New Covenants. John's mission was to announce the coming of Jesus as Messiah (God's anointed) and to baptize Him, thus signifying that He was officially *ordained* by the Father for His public ministry. Not long after He was baptized, Jesus announced that the historical and contemporary aspects of God's redemptive purpose had merged. Exemplary of that fact, Luke recorded the occurrence of an important transitional event.

Jesus visited Nazareth, His hometown and the city where he had been raised. On the sabbath, He went to the synagogue to teach (see Lk. 4:16). In line with Jewish custom, the minister in charge of the service called upon Jesus to read the Scripture. The Torah (Law) portion for that day was the Book of Isaiah. Jesus read from chapter 61, verses 1 through 3:

> *The Spirit of the Lord is upon Me, because He hath anointed Me to preach the gospel to the poor; He hath sent Me to heal the brokenhearted, to preach deliverance to the captives, and recovering of sight to the blind, to set at liberty them that are bruised, to preach the acceptable year of the Lord* (Luke 4:18-19).

Isaiah's prophecy contained the essence of the Kingdom message: *God has developed and executed a plan for restoring broken lives and for repairing the severed fellowship between Himself and fallen man.*

Following His reading of the Scripture, Jesus gave the book back to the minister and sat down. As those in the synagogue watched, Jesus surprised His audience by saying, "...This day is this scripture fulfilled in your ears" (Lk. 4:21). He then announced that God had chosen Him as the messenger of the Kingdom. With that announcement came a new strategy in the advancement of God's redemptive purpose. Salvation would come by God's grace and not by the works of the Law. That strategy continues to be in effect to-day for believing hearts throughout the world.

The Bible does not contain a specific definition of the Kingdom of God. In fact, although Jesus spoke of what the Kingdom is like, He never defined it. What Jesus did, however, was to demonstrate by His own life the two things that make the Kingdom a reality: faith in God and obedience to God. We shall now develop a technical and operational definition of the Kingdom of God.

Defining and Describing the Kingdom of God

From a technical standpoint, we may define the Kingdom of God as *the realm in which God rules and reigns*. Watchman Nee, in his book, *Spiritual Authority*, similarly defines God's Kingdom as "that realm in which the will of God is carried out without any interference" (Nee 1972, 56). Building upon this foundation, we may describe God's Kingdom as a realm, a rule, and a reign.

1. *God's Realm is the area over which He presides*: It is the place of His dominion. It is the geographical and political area that is governed by Almighty God. It represents the breadth, or scope, of His authority.

Every monarch, king, president, or prince exercises political control over a group or nation of people. As such, he or she operates within a particular set of boundaries. These boundaries are established in order to outline the physical area of government, as well as to specify those who are to be governed by that leader. For example, the chief of a small African village may be revered by his tribal constituency, but his authority is limited.

This principle is relevant in the animal world as well. The lion is considered to be king among all beasts, at least on the land. Wherever he roars, he is honored above all other animals. Moreover, within each lion pride, there is a dominant male which establishes the area in which that pride will reside. He has his choice of female mating partners, and the other males in the pride must yield to his rulership in every aspect of community life. In reality, "Mr. Lion" only dominates that area of the jungle that he has marked off and can successfully defend. Again, the breadth of his authority is limited.

God has no limits to his authority. His ruling area is universal. The Bible says, "In the beginning God created the heaven and the earth...and all the host of them" (Gen. 1:1; 2:1). God was responsible for all levels of the whole of creation. He was also the initiator, instigator, and final authority for everything that existed. The once-arrogant Nebuchadnezzar, king of Babylon, after suffering humiliation at the hand of God, was left to say,

And all the inhabitants of the earth are reputed as nothing: and He doeth according to His will in the army of heaven, and among the inhabitants of the earth: and none can stay His hand, or say unto Him, What doest thou? (Daniel 4:35)

Furthermore, David, king of Israel, said, "The earth is the Lord's, and the fulness thereof; the world, and they that dwell therein. For He hath founded it upon the seas, and established it upon the floods" (Ps. 24:1-2). We may say, then, that the Kingdom of God is universal. He is preeminent at all levels and at all times. Since His kingdom is eternal, there will never be a time or place in which God is not God over all.

The scope of God's authority extends throughout the spirit realm (angels, satan, demons, powers, and principalities), the natural realm (the entire animal chain and all organic and inorganic matter), and the human realm. Observe the following:

a. *The Spirit Realm*: God has created, is superior to, and is in control of all spirit beings. These include angels, satan, demons, principalities, powers, and all other spiritual forces in the universe.

Angels, supernatural spirit beings, have been given the responsibility of offering constant praise at the throne of God, in addition to serving as messengers and agents of God across the universe. Throughout biblical history, angels have often appeared on the earth in human form. Therefore, the typical depiction of them as winged creatures, flying about the heavens, delimits the variety of their manifestation among us, even today. That is why the writer in the Book of Hebrews said, "...Be not forgetful to entertain strangers: for thereby some have entertained angels unawares" (Heb. 13:2).

For generations, angels have been used to perform a variety of important functions. "Are they not all ministering spirits, sent forth to minister for them who shall be heirs of salvation?" (Heb. 1:14) In the Book of Revelation, they appear as governors over the seven churches of Asia (see Rev. 2–3). They will be among the "...ten thousand times ten thousand, and thousands of thousands; saying with a loud voice, Worthy is the Lamb that was slain to receive power, and riches, and wisdom, and strength, and honor, and glory, and blessing" (Rev. 5:11-12).

It is certain that angels are not wimps! During the sealing of the servants of God, four of them will be stationed at each of the four corners of the earth, holding back the wind (see Rev. 7:1-3). Only a single angel will be needed to cast satan into a bottomless pit and bind him there for a thousand years (see Rev. 20:1-3).

Satan, who was originally called lucifer, was chief among the angelic host. When he and his cohorts rebelled against God's authority, they were expelled to the outer regions of Heaven (see Is. 14:12-15; Lk. 10:18; Rev. 12:8-9). Satan has been delegated a level of authority by God, and he has been given the freedom to exercise a limited degree of influence in the earth for a specified time. Although he directs and commissions demons and all other evil spirits, he functions under the headship of God. Satan has already been positionally dethroned and will ultimately be destroyed (see Rev. 20:10).

b. *The Natural Realm*: In the six-day Creation, described in Genesis chapter 1, God created the following: the "Day" and the "Night," the heavens and the earth, dry land and waterways, the yield of nature, the sun, moon, stars, and the seasons. God created all living creatures in the water, in the air, and on the land. He established the reproductive process in order to continue the life cycle (see Gen. 1:2-25). All the elements in the natural realm, including both organic and inorganic matter, have been created by, and are under the ultimate control of Almighty God.

God rules in the natural realm. Animals (the entire food chain), although living creatures, are considered part of the natural realm. Even though they possess a soul (mind, will, and emotions), animals have no spirit and are, therefore, not eternal beings. Animals have some reasoning but are devoid of conceptualization. They are incapable, therefore, of making moral judgments.

c. *The Human Realm*: God has created and controls spirit beings. He has ultimate dominion over all of nature. And His authority reaches to the highest level of His creation—the level of the human species. God created both male and female, giving them dominion and stewardship "...over the fish of the sea, and over the fowl of the air, and over the cattle, and over all the earth, and over every creeping thing that creepeth upon the earth" (see also Gen. 1:27-31).

Mankind has been created as a triune being. Each of us is a living spirit (an eternal being), containing a soul (mind, will, and emotions) and inhabiting a physical body. The spirit is the only human component that can be holy. The physical human frame is decaying every day, but the spiritual element will live forever. When God breathed His breath into us, we became alive. Each day that we live, we belong to Him. In Psalm 139, David asked rhetorically,

> *Whither shall I go from Thy spirit? or whither shall I flee from Thy presence? If I ascend up into heaven, Thou art there: if I make my bed in hell, behold, Thou art there. If I take the wings of the morning, and dwell in the uttermost parts of the sea; even there shall Thy hand lead me, and Thy right hand shall hold me* (Psalms 139:7-10).

In the New Testament, Paul said, "For whether we live, we live unto the Lord; and whether we die, we die unto the Lord: whether we live therefore, or die, we are the Lord's" (Rom. 14:8). As part of God's total possessions, we come under His ultimate control.

2. *God's Rule is the degree of His influence within the universe.* God is sovereign over all, which means that He answers to no one but

Himself. He plans and dispenses as He chooses. His thoughts and actions are a result of His own predisposition. He contains the authority, power, and might to execute His desires freely. He has no limitation and is, therefore, able to imagine, say, and do anything!

Operationally, God's rule is expressed in His authority, power, and might. He is King of kings and Lord of lords as well as the sovereign and supreme Ruler of the universe. David, at the height of his own reign over Israel, said of God:

> *Thine, O Lord, is the greatness, and the power, and the glory, and the victory, and the majesty: for all that is in the heaven and in the earth is Thine; Thine is the kingdom, O Lord, and Thou art exalted as head above all* (1 Chronicles 29:11).

The Kingdom of God is a theocracy. His rule is absolute. He requires obedience, not discussion or negotiation.

In the Job 38–42:6, God asks Job some 74 different questions in order to reiterate His absolute sovereignty throughout the universe. Observe a sampling: "Have the gates of death been opened unto thee? or hast thou seen the doors of the shadow of death?" (Job 38:17) "Canst thou send lightnings, that they may go, and say unto thee, Here we are" (Job 38:35) "Doth the hawk fly by thy wisdom, and stretch her wings toward the south? Doth the eagle mount up at thy command, and make her nest on high?" (Job 39: 26-27)

By the time God had finished, Job said, "I have heard of Thee by the hearing of the ear: but now mine eye seeth Thee. Wherefore I abhor myself, and repent in dust and ashes" (Job 42:5-6). Job recognized that in comparison with God, he was worthless. The self-pity that he had felt as a result of losing his family and his natural possessions was replaced with deep reverence for Almighty God. In the end, God gave Job twice as much as he had lost (see Job 42:10).

3. *God's Reign is the process whereby His creation responds to His will*: All levels of creation are ultimately accountable to God. He delegates His authority among the various levels of the universe. God reigns over the spirit and natural realms without dispute or question. The

issue of choice in obeying God's will is exclusive to human beings. And even though we may petition or entreat God, we may not manipulate Him. He does not make deals; He is the standard by which all right exists.

In this component of our analytical model, we shall see a clear distinction among the three realms of the Kingdom. Presently, Heaven is the only place where God's will is performed unobstructedly.

Angelic beings are compelled by the sovereignty and might of God to perform His will exclusively. Although they unceasingly praise and work for God, they do not know Him as Redeemer and Savior because they have never been spiritually lost. I believe that in the beginning, God must have given spirit beings some degree of individual will and power. I say this because had they been purely robotical, satan and others of their kind would have been unable to mutiny in Heaven.

Satan has been referred to as beelzebub, the prince of devils (see Mt. 12:24; Mk. 3:22), the prince of this world (see Jn. 12:31; 14:30; 16:11), and the prince of the power of the air (see Eph. 2:2). All these references assume that he has been given a degree of authority by Almighty God. Although unsuccessful, satan was bold enough to tempt Jesus immediately after He had been ordained of God for His public ministry (see Mt. 4:1-11; Mk. 1:12-13; Lk. 4:1-13). Witchcraft, divination (false prophecy, fortune telling, sorcery, clairvoyance), magic, and some working of miracles, were all practiced in the Old Testament. Most of these situations, except where God directly intervened, operated under the delegated authority of satan.

All powers, spirits, principalities, and forces are subject to the final word of God. These competing forces of ill-will have operated since before the creation of the world. Yet they have always known of, and acknowledged their inferiority to, Almighty God. Daniel prophesied of a future time when God would set up an everlasting Kingdom that would destroy all others (see Dan. 2:44; 7:14).

Announcing that the Kingdom of God had come in Himself, Jesus said, "But if I cast out devils by the Spirit of God, then the kingdom of God is come unto you" (Mt. 12:28). God reigns over spirit beings.

God reigns in the natural realm as well. Inorganic matter has neither spirit nor will. It is ultimately in subjugation to the will of God. The same may be said of organic matter, including the entire animal kingdom. This notwithstanding, the influence of satanic forces may be seen at all levels of God's creational chain.

Destructive phenomena such as earthquakes, floods, and tornadoes occur under the influence of satan, although God uses these phenomena to perform the work of His chastisement of mankind. The changing cycles of the seasons and the operations of nature (i.e. sun, moon, rain, reproduction, the balance of nature, etc.) testify to the fact that most of God's creation is simply out of satan's reach.

God has used members of the animal kingdom to perform various acts of His will. When Pharaoh refused to release the Israelites from his tyrannical rule, God used frogs, flies, and locusts to afflict the Egyptians (see Ex. Chaps. 8–10). He made a donkey talk to Balaam in an effort to draw the Midianite sorcerer's attention to God's direction in his life (see Num. 22:28-30). God also created a great fish to swallow the disobedient Jonah who had refused to obey God's command to prophesy to the city of Ninevah. God then saved Jonah after he repented (see Jon. 1:17; 2:10).

Hundreds of years before it came to pass, Zechariah prophesied of Jesus' triumphal entry into Jerusalem: "...He is just, and having salvation; lowly, and riding upon an ass, and upon a colt the foal of an ass" (Zech. 9:9). That animal was preordained by God to be available for use by Jesus at the precise moment in which it was needed.

Humans are the only part of God's creation capable of exhibiting His character and attributes upon the earth (see Gen. 1:26). We have been created spirit, mind, and body. We are spiritual replicas of God, but naturally, we are Adamic clones. Our spirits are eternal, but our flesh is temporal and of the earth. The part of us which mediates between spirit and body is the mind. The mind is the seat of intelligence, conceptualization, reason, personal will, and emotion. Whatever thoughts are contrived in our minds are generally translated into our behavior.

God knows our thoughts even before we form them. For example, the apostle Paul wrote that the Word of God is "...a discerner of the thoughts and intents of the heart" (Heb. 4:12), meaning that God, through His Holy Scriptures, examines all of our thoughts, including the motives behind them, and judges them in relation to His holy standards.

In the human environment, the Kingdom of God becomes a *partnership*. It is a process of dynamic interaction between God and mankind in which we are provided on-going opportunities to obey our Creator. The Kingdom of God involves people making conscious choices to live and act in accordance with the will of God.

Features of the Kingdom

The Kingdom of God is a reflection of God's nature and character. As such, everything in it is opposite from the natural world view.

First, God's Kingdom is driven by love. God is eternal, all-powerful, all-knowing, and filling all space at all time. And yet, paradoxically, He chooses to rule this universe not by brute force, but by His love! In fact, because God is love (see 1 Jn. 4:8), He is able and willing to invite us into intimate fellowship with Him.

Second, the rules governing God's Kingdom are different from anything we are accustomed to. God operates as the center of all things, and He is the reason for all things. There is no competition among Kingdom dwellers for position or social status.

God sees each of us as we really are, and He alone is qualified to judge, dismiss, or promote us. In His Kingdom, the ditch-digger and the millionaire are the same. The Black man and the White man are the same. There is no innate difference between Christian and Hindu, Buddhist and Jew. The distinction is between those who believe and obey God and those who do not.

Many wars have been fought throughout the centuries, supposedly in the name of God and religion. The only thing that they have proven is that humans are capable of the most heinous thoughts and behaviors. This may seem sacriligious or irreverent, but left on his own, a Christian cannot serve God any easier than a Muslim or a Taoist. Without the operation of the love of God, which we have received in Christ, our destiny is the same as that of the beast of the field: "...all are of the dust, and all turn to dust again" (Eccles. 3:20).

In the Kingdom of God, perfect submission precedes and is a prerequisite for all promotion. The degree of our elevation in the Kingdom is in direct proportion to the extent of our submission to God's will. There are no exceptions. The only way up God's *Kingdom corporate ladder* is to bow to His ultimate authority.

We cannot truly bow to the authority of God without yielding to those whom He has delegated to be over us in some area. We are to be in submission to our government and to our political and civil leaders. God requires us to respect the authority of our legal system, our employers and supervisors, and our spiritual leaders, including pastors and teachers. To live in disobedience to delegated authority is to live in disobedience to God.

A third feature of God's Kingdom is that, although no Kingdom dweller is perfect (sin-free), all who believe and accept Christ as Lord of their lives are considered righteous (in right standing) before the Father. There has never been a person other than Christ who lived completely without sin. However, God's desire is that we each remain open to the process of His workings in us toward the goal of our perfection in Him.

Fourth, the language of the Kingdom is the language of faith. We are to agree with what God says about things. He challenges us to see as He sees and to confess His confession. In the humanistic world, truth may only be established on the basis of a given body of physical evidence. Quantitative, evidentiary proof is the standard for validating every claim that is made; there is no room for faith. In God's Kingdom, however, His Word overrides all the limits of the natural mind. We have but to believe what He says and then to act on that.

Finally, the Kingdom of God is activated *within humankind.* Jesus said, "...The kingdom of God cometh not with observation:

neither shall they say, Lo here! or, lo there! for, behold, the kingdom of God is within you" (Lk. 17:20-21). God's Kingdom is activated on the earth, first in the person of Jesus Christ. He has been given the authority for mediating fellowship between God and man. Under the terms of the New Blood Covenant, all who confess the Lordship of Christ in their lives will be saved, transformed, redeemed, and made righteous before God.

In this "Age of Grace," the Holy Spirit has been charged with the responsibility for implementing the New Covenant provisions. The Spirit is poured out upon believers so that they may form Christ's Church. With the empowerment of the Spirit, the Church is to replicate the mission and ministry of Christ throughout the world. The Kingdom of God also becomes a reality in the life of each person who chooses to walk by faith in obedience to God's will.

Jesus Christ: The Human Prototype of God's Kingdom

Jesus Christ demonstrated the perfect pattern of God's Kingdom: what it is and how it operates. He lived, ministered, and died in perfect obedience to the will of God. On one occasion, Jesus' disciples encouraged Him to take time from His labor to eat a meal, thus renewing His natural strength. But Jesus replied, "...My meat is to do the will of Him that sent Me, and to finish His work" (Jn. 4:34). His passion—the thing that drove Him—involved living in total submission to God.

Jesus struggled, as do we, with the choice between His will and the will of the Father. Facing imminent death, He went to the Garden of Gethsemane and prayed. Expressing His natural, human feelings, Jesus cried, "...Father, if Thou be willing, remove this cup from Me: nevertheless not My will, but Thine, be done" (Lk. 22:42). In accordance with the Father's will, Jesus endured the humiliation of death on a cross at Calvary. He satisfied God's legal requirement for redeeming lost humanity, and for this He was given a name and a position above all others.

Paul said that God raised Christ from the dead and,

...Set Him at his own right hand in the heavenly places, far above all principality, and power, and might, and dominion, and every name that is named, not only in this world, but also in that which is to come: and hath put all things under His feet, and gave Him to be the head over all things to the church, which is His body, the fulness of Him that filleth all in all (Ephesians 1:20-23).

Jesus: The Way Into the Kingdom

Jesus Christ is the door through which all must pass in order to gain direct access to the Father. Jesus announced, "...I am the way, the truth, and the life: no man cometh unto the Father, but by Me" (Jn. 14:6). In Jesus, *Yahweh*, the "I Am" of the Old Covenant, became *Logos* (the living Word) of the New Covenant. Jesus, who was God in the beginning and who was also the Lamb that took away the sins of the world, ascended to the position of Lord of all. As Colson says,

"...Jesus does not claim to be just one truth or one reality among many, but to be the ultimate reality...the root of what is and what was, the point of origin and framework for all that we can see and know and understand. It is the assertion that in the beginning was God, that He is responsible for the universe, for our very existence, and that He has created the order and structure in which life exists. Everything we know...all meaning...flows from Him" (Colson 1992, 152).

Jesus could, therefore, say with confidence, "...no man cometh unto the Father, but by Me." He then stated the requirements for entering God's Kingdom: a change of heart, spiritual rebirth, and childlike faith.

Changing of the heart is the process by which we renounce our previous life of sin and self-dedication and accept God's free gift of salvation. Repentance, the first step in this process, involves our confession that we are sinners and enemies of the cross of Christ, and our agreement to turn toward Christ as our Savior.

Being "born again" involves our recognition that the sovereign and preeminent God has sent Jesus to be the Savior of this world, and then making a confession that Jesus is Lord of our own lives. In the process of the new birth, we exchange our nature and motives for those of Christ. Peter said, "Neither is there salvation in any other: for there is none other name under heaven given among men, whereby we must be saved" (Acts 4:12). Because salvation is a personal matter, individual confession is required. Jesus is Lord because God says so. But He is my Lord because I say so. In Romans 10:9, Paul says, "...if thou shalt confess with thy mouth the Lord Jesus, and shalt believe in thine heart that God hath raised him from the dead, thou shalt be saved."

A beautiful component of the conversion process involves water baptism by immersion in the name of Jesus. Christ told His disciples, "He that believeth and is baptized shall be saved; but he that believeth not shall be damned" (Mk. 16:16). Water baptism is viewed by some as a literal washing or cleansing from sin, required before one can be saved. The Scriptures do not generally support this interpretation. Rather, when one is baptized, he/she is actually making a public confession that Jesus Christ is Lord of his/her life.

In baptism, each candidate demonstrates his/her belief that Jesus, through His death, burial, and resurrection, has paid for every sin that he/she has committed or will ever commit. When one is placed beneath the water, his/her old life is buried with Christ, and he/she arises from the water knowing that a new life has begun in Christ. But water baptism must be seen as *an outward expression of an inward confession*. The act of a person being baptized without verbally confessing the Lordship of Christ in his/her life produces nothing more than a wet sinner. Confession and baptism are joint requirements to conversion and salvation.

Conversion also leads to sanctification, a process in which we are set apart unto God for His service. Although conversion is an instant event that results from God's grace coupled with our faith, sanctification is a process that lasts throughout our lifetime. It occurs as a result of God's constant dealings with us in every aspect of our lives as He works to conform us into the image of Christ.

As a result of conversion and sanctification, we are entitled to receive all the promises that God has made to those who believe in

Jesus Christ, including, but not limited to, being baptized in the Holy Spirit, accompanied by the evident sign of speaking in other tongues as the Spirit gives the utterance (see Acts 2:4).

Finally, exercising childlike faith is the act of accepting the Word of God as truth and then abiding in it. Jesus said,

> *...Suffer little children to come unto Me, and forbid them not: for of such is the kingdom of God. Verily I say unto you, Whosoever shall not receive the kingdom of God as a little child shall in no wise enter therein* (Luke 18:16-17).

Jesus emphasized the fact that our humility before God assures us that He will forgive us, accept us as His own, and exalt us. For example, Jesus stated, "Whosoever therefore shall humble himself as this little child, the same is greatest in the kingdom of heaven" (Mt. 18:4). God readily responds to broken hearts and tender spirits. We can find rest in knowing that He will build us up as we revere Him and live in humble submission to His will.

Conclusion

In this chapter, we have defined the Kingdom of God as the place in which God rules and reigns. We have traced the origin and development of this spiritual concept, examining its nature, how it operates, and how we gain entrance into it. But such an intellectual understanding is not enough. In order for us to make the transition from theory into practice, we need to know how the Kingdom may become a reality in our everyday lives.

Jesus prayed, "Thy kingdom come. Thy will be done in earth, as it is in heaven" (Mt. 6:10). The Kingdom of God is already a reality in Heaven and has been demonstrated on the earth by Jesus Christ through His life, ministry, and perfect sacrifice. The promise of God's eternal Kingdom will only be fulfilled upon completion of His redemptive drama. As we shall see in the final chapter of this text, however, God's Kingdom purpose may be advanced in this present era by a believing humanity that seeks to perform His will in their lives.

Challenge Questions:

1. Does God have the legal right to override our human will?
2. If satan is the "prince of the power of the air," how can we prevent him from contaminating our communications with God?
3. Does the Church have the authority to bring the Kingdom of God into complete fulfillment in this current era?
4. Why is individual verbal confession a key ingredient in the salvation process?
5. Based upon the technical and operational definitions developed in this chapter, are satanists, atheists, and others who reject God exempt from being under His dominion?

References

Colson, Charles, and Ellen Santillii Vaughn. *The Body: Being Light in Darkness*. Dallas, London, Vancouver, Melbourne: Word Publishing, 1992.

Nee, Watchman. *Spiritual Authority*. New York, NY: Christian Fellowship Publishers, Inc., 1972.

Chapter 12

"Let's Get It On!"

And from the days of John the Baptist until now the kingdom of heaven suffereth violence, and the violent take it by force (Matthew 11:12).

I love to watch professional boxing! Despite the ongoing scandals that have left the sport with a tainted image, I remain a loyal, albeit skeptical, fight fan.

As a kid, I grew up watching the "Friday Night Fights" on television with my dad and brothers. Perhaps it was then that I developed the belief that professional boxing is probably the most basic of all athletic contests. Each fighter has the same goal in mind: Beat your opponent into submission or knock him out. The grueling, toe-to-toe battles, requiring superb physical and mental conditioning, are waged without the benefit of modern safety advances. For example, fighters wear no helmets or shoulder pads, and protective gear is limited to a groin cup and a mouthpiece.

I am often amazed by the athletes' combined power, speed, and gracefulness. But I have often wondered while watching the unbridled rage that is unleashed by these finely-tuned fighting machines: *How could such a vicious activity have survived within a civilized society?* And the obvious answer is...money.

My favorite boxing referee is Mills Lane. A judge by profession, Lane prances about the ring skillfully maintaining law and order, a difficult task given the nature of the sport. Before the opening bell, Mills summons the fighters to the center of the ring and in typical judge-like fashion, issues final instructions. He reminds them to obey his commands and to protect themselves at all times. As he directs the two combatants to shake hands, he ends with a resounding "Okay, let's get it on!"

I believe that professional boxing is a lot like Kingdom warfare. It involves the basic principle of "kill or be killed." Maybe that sounds too simple, too vicious. But the way I see it, we, as believers, are not here to tiptoe through life without a struggle. At stake is our eternal future. Let us examine this issue through spiritual eyes.

Kingdom Warfare

Jesus said, "And from the days of John the Baptist until now the kingdom of heaven suffereth violence, and the violent take it by force" (Mt. 11:12). He wanted us to know that the Church is part of the struggle to regain supremacy over God's total creation. The apostle Paul added that we are engaged in a war, not against flesh and blood, but against "...principalities, against powers, against the rulers of the darkness of this world, against spiritual wickedness in high places" (Eph. 6:12). These forces operate under the leadership and influence of satan.

Let there be no doubt—God is in control. For as Moses said, "Even from everlasting to everlasting, Thou art God" (Ps. 90:2b). And although Christ's victory over satan has secured an eternal inheritance for God's posterity, it is unscriptural to say that we have no current earthly conflict. We are engaged in a basic struggle with the forces of darkness. We have but one goal and that is to win! Satan and his army are not waiting patiently and courteously while we train and equip ourselves for battle. Instead, as we stand eyeball to eyeball with the enemy of our souls, we must be prepared to protect ourselves at all times. It is within the context of this struggle that God's Kingdom is advanced as we continuously submit ourselves to His perfect will.

Our Adversary, the Devil

Satan is the archenemy of the Church. He is real, as Christ and heaven are real, and he represents the ultimate driving force behind all spiritual attacks. He contended with God for the allegiance of Adam and Eve in the Garden of Eden. At the moment that they committed high treason against God, satan made the mistake of thinking that he had become the lord of humankind.

The apostle Peter described satan as, "...your adversary the devil [who walks about], as a roaring lion...seeking whom he may devour" (1 Pet. 5:8). James said that we must resist satan before he will flee from us, which presumes that he has some sphere of influence, even today (see Jas. 5:7). Paul, emphasizing satan's ability to influence us, referred to him as the "...prince of the power of the air, the spirit that now worketh in the children of disobedience" (Eph. 2:2).

It is incorrect, therefore, to say that satan is powerless. However, as we determined in the previous chapter of this text, satan is operating under a limited amount of God-given authority. For God is all-powerful, and satan is not. God knows everything, but satan's knowledge is finite. God is universally present all the time, but satan is not. What, then, makes satan such a formidable foe, and what are his primary weapons?

Satan's Arsenal

Satan cannot kill us—that is, the spiritual part of us—because death is no longer in his hands. Our lives are hidden in Christ, who defeated satan almost 2,000 years ago. But if satan can neither kill nor defeat us, then what can he do? He can still attack our physical bodies. He can initiate and spread disease and torment of every kind. In addition, he can create the situational chaos that causes nations to war against one another. But how can satan do that?

I believe that satan's biggest weapon is deception. He capitalizes on the fact that we simply do not know God as we should and that we do not know satan for the deceiver that he is. As a result, he gains tremendous leverage in our lives, and he uses it to influence our motives, thoughts, and behaviors.

Satan is more than a toothless lion. He exploits our ignorance concerning our identity in Christ, and he attacks us with a spirit of fear and unbelief. He further victimizes us by stirring up division among us and by stifling our ability to dream.

The Struggle Within

Satan is not an unbeatable foe. For, as the apostle John said, "...greater is He [Christ] that is in you, than he [satan] that is in the world" (1 Jn. 4:4). This notwithstanding, we frequently become unwitting participants in satan's efforts to defeat us. It seems that the major threat to our success in God lies in our potential unwillingness to yield to His will. It is the conscious choice that we make to operate in the context of our own humanistic senses rather than to walk by faith. Please allow an explanation.

Human reasoning is not automatically in contradiction to God. In fact, He has endowed us with the intelligence and faith to investigate and solve problems. The capacity of the human mind exceeds that of the most advanced computers.

There are numerous examples of the successful partnership between God and humankind, much beyond the scope of this text. We have defeated many diseases that were at one time thought to be incurable. We have split the atom. We have learned to transplant human organs. We have explored outer space. Therefore, the human mind is not a natural enemy of its Creator. The human mind and will form, instead, a proving ground for the exercise of our faith. Even after our spiritual new birth, however, our spirits are constantly engaged in a battle with our natural faculties to gain control over our own motives, thoughts, and behaviors.

Although the New Testament does not imply that believers are immune to all negative influences, some persons still say that our baptism into Christ inoculates us against falling back into sin. Those who take this position argue that, because we have received a new nature (the nature of Christ), it is impossible for us to violate God's law. We are sin-free and, therefore, perfect in every way. I believe that this argument is based upon a misunderstanding of the Scriptures in this regard.

Following our conversion and Spirit baptism, we are empowered with the ability to accomplish all that God has ordained for us.

But our ability to live in the fulfillment of God's purpose is tempered by our *willingness to be led by His Spirit*. Paul addressed the fact that as part of the human dilemma, our natural, human will is at variance with the will of God. Particularly, in Romans chapters 7 and 8, he stated that believers are not spiritual robots. We still retain our God-given right to live in submission to His will or to refuse. In distinguishing between those who walk by faith and those who do not, Paul said:

> *For they that are after the flesh do mind the things of the flesh; but they that are after the Spirit the things of the Spirit. For to be carnally* [naturally] *minded is death; but to be spiritually minded is life and peace. Because the carnal mind is enmity against God: for it is not subject to the law of God, neither indeed can be. So then they that are in the flesh cannot please God* (Romans 8:5-8).

We cannot live in the victory of the cross of Christ without the empowerment of the Holy Spirit. But even with that empowerment, we must be willing to follow the Spirit's leading in our lives.

There is a level in God that we cannot attain, except by faith. The prophet Habakkuk said that, beyond our ability to investigate, to examine, and to understand, "...the just shall live by his faith" (Hab. 2:4; see also Rom. 1:17; Gal. 3:11). Paul repeated this theme in his writing to the Corinthian church. He stated, "For we walk by faith, not by sight" (2 Cor. 5:7). Both Habakkuk and Paul were speaking to God's people and they were telling us to believe God. Again, Paul said, "...as many as are led by the Spirit of God, they are the sons of God" (Rom. 8:14). The term, *sons of God* is derived from the Greek word *huios* denoting those who are developing the *character* of Christ as a result of intimate fellowship with Him.

We can live as God wants us to live. We can be what He wants us to be. It is a matter of our choice! We cannot be destroyed, for our lives are hidden in Christ. With victory promised and secured, our challenge is not to defeat satan or the world, but to believe God. We have been equipped with a spiritual arsenal that allows us to overcome anything that challenges our success in God and, therefore, in life.

The Weapons of Our Warfare

Spiritual warfare cannot be waged with flesh and blood, but with the arsenal that God has placed at our disposal in the realm of the spirit. Paul stated that the weapons of our warfare are not carnal (not restricted by natural or material forces), but they are spiritual. He explained that they are,

> *...mighty through God to the pulling down of strong holds; casting down imaginations, and every high thing that exalteth itself against the knowledge of God, and bringing into captivity every thought to the obedience of Christ* (2 Corinthians 10:4-5).

In Ephesians 6:14-17, Paul again told us to "...take unto you the whole armour of God, that ye may be able to withstand in the evil day...." He described the elements of our spiritual armament as follows:

- *Truth to girt about our loins*: We must guard our hearts. We must know who God is, who we are in Him, what He has given us in Christ, what He requires from us in this life, and what we may expect from Him, both now, and in ages to come;
- *The breastplate of righteousness*: Our motives must be pure. We are to love God and people the way that Jesus taught and demonstrated;
- *The footwear of the preparation of the gospel of peace:* We must see the Church as one body. There can be no room in our worship or our witness for divisiveness. We must share in God's vision that mankind be reconciled to Him through belief in and submission to Christ;
- *The shield of faith:* We will be protected against the onslaughts and eternal destruction of satan to the degree that we believe and trust in God's Word. Therefore, we must be firmly planted and established in Him;

- *The helmet of salvation*: We must be convinced of the Lordship of Christ and willing to elevate Him to the preeminent position in our lives;
- *The sword of the Spirit* (God's Word): Spiritual warfare can only take place in the spirit realm. The only thing that pierces the forces of darkness consistently and completely is God's Word. Ultimately, it is the Word of God that protects us, corrects us, heals us, perfects us, and guarantees our complete victory in Christ.

Enclothed with God's heavenly armor, we are able to fight successfully against all principalities, powers, rulers of darkness, and spiritual wickedness in high places. Speaking through Isaiah, God made a solemn and irrevocable promise:

No weapon that is formed against thee shall prosper; and every tongue that shall rise against thee in judgment thou shalt condemn. This is the heritage of the servants of the Lord, and their righteousness is of Me, saith the Lord (Isaiah 54:17).

We have God's Word that we cannot fail. We will walk in complete victory as we live in submission to His authority and as we utilize our spiritual arsenal.

The apostle John described his vision of the endtimes:

And I heard a loud voice saying in heaven, Now is come salvation, and strength, and the kingdom of our God, and the power of His Christ: for the accuser of our brethren is cast down, which accused them before our God day and night. And they overcame him by the blood of the Lamb, and by the word of their testimony; and they loved not their lives unto the death (Revelation 12:10-11).

The angel was telling John about Christ's Church! He was telling John that he saw us defeating satan, whose ultimate demise is predetermined by Almighty God.

In spite of his continuing attacks against us, satan is already defeated. Furthermore, he knows the difference between those whom he must fear and those whom he can bluff! He is not prepared to face the advance of a Church that is empowered by the Holy Spirit and that is full of faith. He knows that God's Kingdom is advanced by a people who are praying to and trusting in God on a daily basis.

How to Pursue the Kingdom

The Kingdom of God is not a vague theoretical construct, impossible to apply in the real world. It is a dynamic process whereby we yield our lives to God in our daily walk. Below is a set of fundamental, Bible-based principles that when applied will help us to pursue God's Kingdom. None should come as a surprise (see Fig. 12.1).

(Fig. 12.1) **PURSUING THE KINGDOM OF GOD**

1. *We must first obey God's Law.* In Judaism, there are 613 laws and commandments. All are derived from and based upon the Ten Commandments, the principles contained in the Law of Moses. During the time of Christ, the Pharisees and other legalists stressed

the importance of living in strict adherence to the Mosaic Law, and although they gave lip service to this requirement, they lived hypocritically.

a. *The Greatest Commandment*: A man once asked Jesus, "...which is the great commandment in the law?" (Mt. 22:36) Jesus knew that the man was attempting to snare Him in a legalistic trap. Therefore, in His reply, Jesus synthesized the spirit and intent of the Law:

> *...Thou shalt love the Lord thy God with all thy heart, and with all thy soul, and with all thy mind. This is the first and great commandment. And the second is like unto it, Thou shalt love thy neighbour as thyself. On these two commandments hang all the law and the prophets* (Matthew 22:37-40).

According to Jesus, our top two priorities in life must be to love God and to love people (see Deut. 6:5; Lev. 19:18)! Everything else is based upon these two principles.

God's preeminent law of love is given, not as an option, but as a requirement. The apostle John said that a man is a liar if he claims to love God and yet continues to hate his brother (see 1 Jn. 4:20). We are encouraged to love those who are in the family of God, without regard for their particular denominational preference. Religious and doctrinal differences aside, the Holy Spirit baptizes us into Christ's Body, which is one. For this reason, division and separation cannot be embraced as a normal pattern of the Church's functioning. Paul said, "For by one Spirit are we all baptized into one body, whether we be Jews or Gentiles, whether we be bond or free; and have been all made to drink into one Spirit" (1 Cor. 12:13).

Either we are truly a family and we will strive to minister to one another, or we are not a family at all and, therefore, not of Christ. This is an issue of particular importance to those of us in the Pentecostal Movement. God has given us the opportunity to operate as a unique and refreshing component of the Body of Christ. We must begin by building bridges of love and fellowship between ourselves and those in the larger Christian community.

b. *Loving Our Enemies*: Beyond the requirement that we love one another, Christians have a particular biblical responsibility to love—not just accept or tolerate—those who are outside the Christian community. This includes loving our enemies! Jesus denounced the "spiritual in-breeding" that is prevalent within the Church today, by saying, "...Love your enemies, bless them that curse you, do good to them that hate you, and pray for them which despitefully use you, and persecute you" (Mt. 5:44). Paul later stated, "...if thine enemy hunger, feed him; if he thirst, give him drink..." (Rom. 12:20). This inclusive mandate may seem impossible to meet, but if we fail to obey God in this area—the area of love—then nothing else that we do really matters.

Love is dynamic. It begins with an attitude, and it ends with an act. God loved us so much that He gave His Son in order to purchase our salvation. That sacrificial gesture established a principle by which we are to live all the time. Loving requires giving, and those who would love the best must give the most.

2. *We must walk by faith and not by sight.* Faith is the pathway into God's presence. The Book of Hebrews states, "Now faith is the substance of things hoped for, the evidence of things not seen" (Heb. 11:1). I believe that faith is simply this: *the ability and willingness to agree with God.* By His grace, we receive the faith required in order to gain access to Him. Although it is always available for our use, faith must be put into practice. Faith that is dormant is like an unused muscle or brain cell. It is like being in a darkened room and never turning on the light switch.

a. *Increasing our faith*: I do not share the view of some that faith can be or should be increased quantitatively. More prayer, more fasting, or more consecration will not produce more faith. I believe that when we receive the life of God's grace in us, we have all the faith necessary for accomplishing whatever He has assigned to us. On the surface, Jesus appears to contradict this position when He asks His disciples, "...Why are ye so fearful? how is it that ye have no faith?" (Mk. 4:40) But Jesus did not admonish His followers for the amount of faith they had, rather for the limited degree to which they used it.

b. *Increasing our fellowship*: We can develop a greater understanding about faith through concentrated and disciplined study of God's Word. We can also expand the scope of our belief when exposed to an environment in which faith is widely practiced. But faith only *grows* in us as a result of our intimate experience with Christ. Fellowship with Jesus Christ is based upon our consistent pursuit of His will. For that reason, beyond our intellectual awareness, beyond our initial expressions of faith, we must be willing to trust Him.

3. *We must trust God for everything.* Paul said, "But my God shall supply all your need according to His riches in glory by Christ Jesus" (Phil. 4:19). Although faith takes us into God's presence, trust moves us into His heart. Trusting God is the real catalyst for growing faith. It is a distinct dimension of our relationship with Him.

a. *Trust is experiential*: Faith is a free gift of God's grace. It is present with us at birth and is perfected within us as we hear the Word of God (see Rom. 10:17). Trust, on the other hand, is experiential. It is a mutual process in which we gain greater confidence in God and He, in turn, reveals Himself more to us. This level of fellowship requires nurturing on our part, and it only develops as we walk with God over an extended period of time. According to Scripture, God is the only One who is worthy of our complete trust, even beyond that given to family, friends, and other associates. The prophet Micah said,

> *Trust ye not in a friend, put ye not confidence in a guide: keep the doors of thy mouth from her that lieth in thy bosom. For the son dishonoureth the father, the daughter riseth up against her mother, the daughter-in-law against her mother-in-law; a man's enemies are the men of his own house. Therefore, I will look unto the Lord; I will wait for the God of my salvation: my God will hear me* (Micah 7:5-7).

b. *Trusting God builds our confidence in Him*: Trust is an instrument that we may use to develop accurate expectations about the future based upon our previous encounters with God. Whenever the future brings us into situations for which we have no explanation,

ill be confident that God is holding us firm. Rather than
additional situations in which to test God's ability, trust provides opportunities to learn more about His life and purpose. The prophet Jeremiah said, "Blessed is the man that trusteth in the Lord, and whose hope the Lord is. For he shall be as a tree planted by the waters, and that spreadeth out her roots by the river…" (Jer. 17:7-8). The more we learn to trust God, the more the integrity of His Word will be confirmed within us.

Faith without trust limits the extent to which we can receive from God. It encourages us to build a fantasy world that is filled with unceasing expectations, rather than to develop greater confidence in God. Faith always confesses that God is and that He rewards those who diligently seek Him (see Heb 11:6), and trust allows us to maintain a conviction that God will do what He says because He is God. Should He choose to perform in a manner other than what we expect, our trust keeps us balanced and prevents us from becoming faint-hearted. I am reminded of the words of the powerful hymn:

> Tis so sweet to trust in Jesus, just to take Him at His word;
> Just to rest upon His promise, just to know thus saith the Lord.
> Jesus, Jesus, how I trust Him, how I've proved Him o'er and o'er;
> Jesus, Jesus, precious Jesus; oh, for grace to trust Him more
>   (Stead, 1882).

c. *The results of not trusting*: As stated above, trusting God helps us to maintain our spiritual balance. With that in mind, I should like to draw attention to two types of errors that may hinder our development in God. Occupying opposite ends of a continuum, each one arises from our efforts to follow God intellectually without trusting in Him to author and finish (develop) our faith.

I call the first type of error *speculation*. A shotgun approach to maintaining our walk with God, speculation is like playing the lottery. We may buy a ticket every week, but we will still be surprised if we ever win anything. Speculation causes us to ask "what if" questions: "What if God really can do what the Bible says that He can?" "What would happen if we were to ask Him to do something for us?" Speculation causes us to experiment with God. It leads us to pray with "one eye open," as we look for God to respond. Faith mixed with trust prevents this type of doubting.

I refer to the second type of error caused by trying to apply faith without trusting God as *presumption*. The presumptive attitude is demonstrated by our attempts to press God into action based solely upon our limited knowledge of His character. When utilized by us, presumption writes a check for some idea or belief and then demands that God cash it.

Presumption leads us to say, "According to the Bible, whatever we ask of God in His name, He will do. We are asking now according to His Word, and therefore, what we are asking for must come to pass." Because presumption is based upon human knowledge of a holy God, it places Him inside the parameters of our understanding, and it leaves Him no room to say "No," or to keep silent. In short, a presumptive attitude dishonors the sovereignty of God.

The ineffectiveness of these two strategies may be simply stated. Speculation does not challenge God because it is not based upon faithful belief. On the other hand, presumption does not force or intimidate God, for He has nothing to prove.

d. *Fueling our faith*: Trusting God fuels our faith as gasoline fuels an automobile. We may admire the styling and beauty of a particular luxury car with its tremendous power and performance potential. It may be equipped with the latest options for comfort, but without fuel it cannot be driven. It sits motionless and idle. Admittedly, we could set that car at the top of a steep hill, put it in neutral, and take off the brake. Even without fuel, it would coast to the bottom. But once there, that same car could not be driven back up the hill without fueling it first.

The Bible states fundamentally that we cannot please God without faith. That is how we begin a relationship with Him. But our intimate fellowship with God is both increased and enhanced as we learn to trust in Him. In the process of our learning, we develop a greater confidence that we cannot fail because we are in Him. Thus, we may take note of another Kingdom principle: *Trusting God takes us to a place in Him where faith alone could never go.*

4. *We must be led by the Holy Spirit.* Living under the guidance and direction of the Holy Spirit is not something that comes naturally to us. It is very much a learned response. After we are baptized in the Holy Spirit and we become infused with the power of the living Christ, we must develop a clear understanding of the Spirit's role in the New Testament Church and in the life of each believer. And there is more.

a. *Developing right motives*: No gift of revelation is needed in order for us to know that God uses His Word as a tool for exposing the root motives that drive our every act (see Heb. 4:12). In fact, "Neither is there any creature that is not manifest in His sight: but all things are naked and opened unto the eyes of Him with whom we have to do" (Heb. 4:13). For this reason, we must pray with David, who knowing that righteous behavior can only come as a result of righteous motivation, said, "Create in me a clean heart, O God; and renew a right spirit within me" (Ps. 51:10).

Although this issue is important for all believers, it is particularly significant for those in leadership positions. Hence, a kingdom principle: *One of the most critical challenges facing spiritual leaders is to discern whether or not their intentions are in alignment with the character and motives of God.* (See Mark 14:35-36; Luke 22:42.) Jesus, acting as our preeminent role model, stated with no hesitation,

> *For I came down from heaven, not to do Mine own will, but the will of Him that sent Me. And this is the Father's will which hath sent Me, that of all which He hath given Me I should lose nothing, but should raise it up again at the last day* (John 6:38-39).

Jesus told His disciples that after they had been filled with the Holy Spirit, they would become able witnesses of His power and life throughout the world (see Acts 1:8). That same promise applies to us as we agree by faith to follow the Spirit's leading in all aspects of our lives. A valid Christian witness includes our willingness to share in the ongoing work of Christ to build His Kingdom. That requirement can only be met as we sacrifice our own selfish motives for the sake of God's desires.

b. *Praying in the Spirit*: A helpful practice in learning how to be Spirit-led is for us to spend a portion of each day praying in tongues, a unique and edifying form of our worship to God. Praying under the inspiration of the Holy Spirit renews and refreshes us, and it fortifies our faith (see Tit. 3:5; Jude 1:20). Paul explained that through this process, we learn to allow the Spirit to intercede for us at the throne of God. As the Holy Spirit uses our tongues to communicate with the Father in languages and in thought processes that are not common to us, we are enabled to pray the will of God in our lives (see Rom. 8:26-27).

c. *Developing spiritual sensitivity*: The importance of consecration and disciplined study of God's Word was already mentioned in this text. Additionally, as we become more sensitive to the gentle urgings of the Holy Spirit, we will discover the numerous ways in which God is intimately concerned about us and about others. Spiritual sensitivity on our part motivates us to stay on "ready alert," listening for the continual teaching, cautioning, comforting, and guiding that the Holy Spirit gives us. We are also aided in our ability to see ourselves in the mirrored image of God's glory and as a result, to practice living after the pattern of Jesus Christ.

5. *We must live to serve.* Pursuing God's Kingdom involves our agreement to take upon ourselves the attitudes of servants. In this generation, service to others is usually the last thing on our minds. Most of the time, we want to be recognized, promoted, and exalted. But Peter said, "Humble yourselves therefore under the mighty hand of God, that He may exalt you in due time" (1 Pet. 5:6).

a. *The image of servanthood*: Quite often, our visions of Christ feature Him walking up and down the shores of Galilee, feeding huddled masses, turning water into wine, and putting demons to flight. Although these images are accurate, they do not cancel out the scene of Jesus, the Son of God, laying aside His garments and His sacred authority, girding himself with a towel, and washing His disciples' feet (see Jn. 13:4-10). Neither do they nullify the fact of the crucifixion where a sinless Christ became sin for us in order that we might become righteous before God.

The *exaltation* of Christ came as a result of, and not before, His *humiliation*. He was, therefore, qualified to say,

> *...but whosoever will be great among you, let him be your minister; and whosoever will be chief among you, let him be your servant: even as the Son of man came not to be ministered unto, but to minister, and to give His life a ransom for many* (Matthew 20:26-28).

If we cannot serve like Christ, then we cannot reign with Him. Jesus said that anyone desiring to become a partaker in His ministry must, "...deny himself, and take up his cross daily, and follow Me" (Lk. 9:23).

b. *Thy will be done*: Paul charged us to present ourselves (body, mind, and spirit) as living sacrifices unto God, set aside and willing to be used as He chooses (see Rom. 12:1-2). We can only prove our love and dedication to God by living in continual obedience to His will. Our confession must echo that of Christ: "...nevertheless not My will, but Thine, be done" (Lk. 22:42).

These are the major elements of our pursuit of the Kingdom of God: obeying God's law, walking by faith, trusting God, being led by the Holy Spirit, and living in service to God and to others. Although it may take only a few minutes to read this list, the requirements included herein will take a lifetime for us to perform. They cannot be mastered in the strength of our own will, and yet they require our will to make them a reality.

The Bible says, "I can do all things through Christ which strengtheneth me" (Phil. 4:13). Therefore, we can be confident that God is on our side and that our victory is guaranteed in the power of His might. We will make it! And now, a final challenge to my fellow Pentecostals and Charismatics.

"The Power of One"

The Church was born in the city of Jerusalem on the Day of Pentecost. As the wind of the Holy Spirit began to blow, crowds gathered in amazement to hear 120 believers praising God in a variety of languages. The apostle Peter preached the first gospel sermon in which he proclaimed both the Lordship of Jesus Christ and the prophetic outpouring of the Holy Spirit upon humanity. The impact of the message was great, the results immediate. Those who heard the preacher's words were stricken with conviction and clamoured to receive God's blessing. That same day, 3,000 souls were baptized in the Holy Spirit. A few days later, another 5,000 were added, and the Pentecostal revival was officially begun.

Today, almost 2,000 years later, the Pentecostal/Charismatic Movement is the fastest-growing Christian belief system in the world. About 400 million persons from numerous cultural, ethnic, racial, and religious backgrounds now embrace Holy Spirit baptism as the highest expression of their conversion experience. As the Spirit is poured out among more nations throughout the world, Jesus continues to give two commands: To the lost, He says, *"COME"*: "Come unto Me all ye that labor, and are heavy laden, and I will give you rest" (Mt. 11:28). But to the Church, He says, *"GO"*: "...Go ye into all the world, and preach the gospel to every creature" (Mk. 16:15). As we go, we must proceed in the power, strength, and unity of Jesus Christ.

The Church is Christ's, henceforth, now, and forever! If it becomes exclusively Pentecostal/Charismatic in nature, then it will no longer be Christ's. There is no "Pentecostal Church" in Heaven, anymore than there is a Methodist or a Baptist one. The Church is not "Presbyterian." It's name is not "Full Gospel" or "Catholic." We were not called by John Calvin or the Wesleys. We were not redeemed by the blood of the martyrs or of Luther, Seymour, Parham, or of our bishop, *but of Christ!*

We, as baptized believers, are challenged, therefore, to look beyond our own denominational and ecclesiastical boundaries. We must take the lead in offering the olive branch of peace to those around us who embrace Christ. We must be the first to confess that, "There is neither Jew nor Greek, there is neither bond nor free, there is neither male nor female: for [we] are all one in Christ Jesus" (Gal. 3:28).

We will press God's Kingdom forward as we fight against all division and divisiveness. We can reduce the number of separate Pentecostal/Charismatic denominations from its current 14,000 down to one. But in order to accomplish that and other unifying tasks, we must develop a new zeal for restoring to the Church her former glory.

It no longer matters who or what we were before our salvation. But now, because of Christ, we are redeemed, transformed, called out, chosen, and sent forth in the "power of One." As Paul has told us, "For as the body is one, and hath many mambers, and all the members of that one body, being many, are one body: so also is Christ" (I Cor. 12:12).

There is only:

One God, who is preeminent Father, living Christ, and Holy Spirit; there is one spotless Lamb, one living Word, one blood sacrifice, one Way, one Truth, one Life, one Door, one Savior/Sanctifier, one Healer, one Baptizer in the Holy Spirit, one King of kings and Lord of lords; there is one faith, one baptism, one salvation, one Church, which is the one Body of Christ, one holy nation, one royal priesthood, and one eternal and everlasting Kingdom of God.

Now, "Kingdom Warriors," let's get it on!

Challenge Questions

1. If satan is already defeated, why should we have to struggle to defeat him?
2. Given that Pentecostals are greatly divided over many theological and practice issues, how can we wage effective warfare against the powers of darkness?
3. What might be some specific strategies for making certain that we are sufficiently armed for spiritual warfare?
4. Is the "whole armour of God" to be used in offensive strategies, defensive ones, or both?
5. Why does the God kind of love require service to others?

Reference

Stead, Louisa M.R., " 'Tis So Sweet to Trust in Jesus," 1882.

Epilogue

It has taken 18 months for me to write this book. It has doubt-less been the most challenging task that I have ever performed. And now, I have such a sense of peace knowing that I have done my best, thus being true to the purpose of God in my life. In reflecting back upon the beginning of this process, when the book was just an idea (more precisely, several disconnected ideas), I am honored that God has chosen to use me in His creative enterprise.

During the creation of this document, I have been changed in many ways. First, I have been forced to reexamine every major value that I hold dear. I have had to alter and clarify previously held ideas and opinions in the light of God's continuing revelation. For example, there were things concerning God, about which I was ab-solutely certain, even though I did not know why. But as a result of God's instruction, I find that I really did not know Him like I thought. Second, I have had to sharpen my skills at becoming a critical thinker, and in the process, I have discovered that in many ways, I was not a thinker at all. I have not become more skeptical about the existence of absolute truth. I have, however, taken full re-sponsibility for faithfully examining those things that I hear, accept, and present to others as being absolute truths. I believe that God is honored by this.

Third, I have discovered afresh the benefit that is derived from the disciplined pursuit of goals. The joy of winning a battle or a con-test is certainly no greater than the pleasure of knowing that we have fought well. A fourth and related change is this: I now realize that the quality time we spend with God may cause us to be alone, but it will never allow us to be lonely. I must join the Psalmist in saying unto God, "...in Thy presence is fulness of joy; at Thy right hand there are pleasures for evermore" (Ps. 16:11).

Probably the greatest impact of this project upon me has been that I have come to appreciate the vastness of God's love. There is so much room in His heart for those who want to be in fellowship with Him, and He has gone to great lengths in providing the opportunity for all who desire to be included in His family. I have already reviewed in this text (Chapter 2) how God has enabled me to recapture my purpose in Him. I am a beneficiary of His immeasurable mercy and grace.

There are times when God seems to act in an exclusive manner, but even His exclusiveness is based upon an inclusive motive. For example, God often separates us to Himself, not so that we will become elitists thinking that we are above everyone else, but so that He might prepare us to effectively witness for Him among those whom He has chosen for us to serve.

I am convinced that Heaven holds an inexhaustible source of authority, power, and grace, and that these are available to those who will pursue God. But the entitlements to His storehouse are not earmarked for a particular sectarian group. As a Pentecostal, I am excited about the baptism in the Holy Spirit. It is certainly a major key for use in unlocking the door to the abundant life in Christ. However, Spirit baptism is not an end unto itself. Instead, it is a means to the end that we might be like Christ. I pray that as we in the Pentecostal Movement, remain excited about the Pentecostal experience and way of life, we will concurrently build bridges of greater understanding and cooperation between us and the rest of Christ's Body, the Church.

I believe that the triumphant Church will advance at a rate never before seen. She will rise up and glorify God throughout the earth. But because of the importance of that mission, the act of engaging in continuous—often meaningless—debate about the superiority of specific theologies or denominations is no longer a valuable use of our time. We have reached the hour when the Church, firmly planted upon the foundation of the living Christ, must take a unified stand against the kingdoms of darkness.

Within the pages of this text, I have attempted to provide some enlightenment on what might seem to be rather obscure issues. I have sought not to be repetitious of those who have preceded me. Still, I have found myself plowing over soil that has been tilled by faithful men and women in ages past. But perhaps it is common that in our pursuit of the things of God, we may cover the same ground many times over before we finally get it right. In our wanderings to find new truth—new revelation—we often stumble over things that should have been obvious to us all along.

In the final analysis, there can be no greater revelation than this: "For God so loved the world, that He gave His only begotten Son, that whosoever believeth in Him should not perish, but have everlasting life" (Jn. 3:16). It is this passage that Martin Luther referred to as "the Bible in miniature," for it summarizes the principle of God's greatest legacy—the legacy of love. And now, a closing prayer:

Father, I feel such joy that You have used me as an instrument in Your hand. I have done my best to represent Your purpose in this, Your creation. May this text be used as a tool in the hands of believing men and women who are seeking to bring Your will and way to this earth. This I ask in the name of Jesus Christ. Amen.

Glossary

Adjure—To command or entreat.

Anointing—God's authorization and empowerment that enables an individual or group to fulfill a particular calling or work, in the accomplishment of His will.

Antithesis—A contrast or opposition of thoughts. The exact opposite.

Apostolic Pentecostalism—A system of belief that emphasizes the teachings of the apostles as the rule for Pentecostal believers.

Attestation—The act of attesting; testimony.

Bequeath—To leave (property) to another by last will and testament. To hand down or pass on.

Capricious—Flighty, subject to change.

Churchese—Church talk. "The language peculiar to the Evangelical culture."

Consummate—To complete or perfect in every way; to bring to fruition.

Covenant—The promise made by God to man.

Dominion—Rule or power to rule. Sovereignty.

Efficacious—Effective. Producing or capable of producing the desired effect.

Evangelical—Referring to a belief in the inspiration and authority of the Bible, with particular emphasis on the need for personal conversion and regeneration by the Holy Spirit.

Fellowship—Intimate and mutual trust between God and individuals.

Glory—The manifested presence of God.

Grace—The total resource of God that He freely gives to an undeserving humanity.

Great Tribulation—A prescribed period following the Rapture when God will pour out His wrath upon the earth.

Heaven—The place of God's abode.

Historicity—Historical validity. The condition of having actually occurred in history.

Human Holiness—Separated unto God for His purpose. Mankind's attempt to meet the standard of a Holy God.

Inerrant—Truth without error of any kind.

Millennial Reign—The thousand-year reign of Christ on the earth, generally believed to occur after the Rapture and the Great Tribulation.

Paradigm—A theoretical model. A conceptual frame of reference.

Particularity—Individuality, as opposed to generality or universality.

Pentecost—"Fiftieth," a name for the harvest feast that occurred 50 days after Passover; refers to the outpouring of the Holy Spirit that occurred 50 days following the resurrection of Jesus Christ.

Pentecostal Movement—The movement that began in 1901 that emphasizes the experience of the baptism in the Holy Spirit, as evidenced by speaking in other tongues and the restoration of the gifts of the Holy Spirit; the spirit and practice of the Pentecostal doctrine and lifestyle.

Preeminent—Eminent above and excelling beyond others. Having no equal.

Progenitor—A forefather. A source from which something develops. The originator or precursor.

Purpose—The specific intention of God to accomplish His will. When known, it becomes man's plan of action.

Rapture—The "snatching" away of the true believers for a meeting with Jesus in the air.

Reconciliation—The restoration of mankind to fellowship with God.

Redemption—The act of buying back. The work of Christ in which He reclaimed mankind from the dominion of satan.

Repentance—A change of attitude toward God involving a turning away from sin and a seeking of God's rule in one's life.

Revelation—The unfolding by God of His character and His will to mankind.

Sovereignty—God's right to be and to do whatever pleases Him.

Testament—A will. The assignment by God of His inheritance to mankind.

Testator—One who has made a will. One who has died leaving a valid will.

Torah—Hebrew, meaning, "instruction" or "teaching." The word from God. It refers generally to the whole Jewish Bible and specifically to the Pentateuch (the first five books).

Worship—The attitude and act of acknowledging God. Yielding one's will to God. Bowing to the fact that He is God.